Pirates

Ross Kemp is the author of *Gangs*, *Gangs II* and *Ross Kemp on Afghanistan*. A familiar face on TV, he has spent the last five years making hard-hitting documentaries around the world.

Pirates

ROSS KEMP

MICHAEL JOSEPH
an imprint of
PENGUIN BOOKS

MICHAEL JOSEPH

Published by the Penguin Group
Penguin Books Ltd, 80 Strand, London WC2R ORL, England
Penguin Group (USA) Inc., 375 Hudson Street, New York, New York 10014, USA
Penguin Group (Canada), 90 Eglinton Avenue East, Suite 700, Toronto, Ontario, Canada M4P 2Y3
(a division of Pearson Penguin Canada Inc.)
Penguin Ireland, 25 St Stephen's Green, Dublin 2, Ireland
(a division of Penguin Books Ltd)
Penguin Group (Australia), 250 Camberwell Road, Camberwell, Victoria 3124, Australia
(a division of Pearson Australia Group Pty Ltd)
Penguin Books India Pvt Ltd, 11 Community Centre, Panchsheel Park, New Delhi – 110 017, India
Penguin Group (NZ), 67 Apollo Drive, Rosedale, North Shore 0632, New Zealand
(a division of Pearson New Zealand Ltd)
Penguin Books (South Africa) (Pty) Ltd, 24 Sturdee Avenue,
Rosebank, Johannesburg 2196, South Africa

Penguin Books Ltd, Registered Offices: 80 Strand, London WC2R ORL, England

www.penguin.com

First published 2009
1

Set in 13.5/16pt Monotype Garamond Std
Typeset by Penguin Books Ltd
Printed in Great Britain by Clays Ltd, St Ives plc

A CIP catalogue record for this book is available from the British Library

ISBN: 978-0-718-15598-8

'Where there is a sea, there are pirates.'
Greek proverb

'It is when pirates count their booty that
they become mere thieves.'
William Bolitho

'The sea was so vast. The vessels they sailed in were
small. Yet still the [pirates] tracked them down . . .'
Linda Colley, *Captives*

Contents

PART 4
Djibouti

PART I
The Gulf of Aden

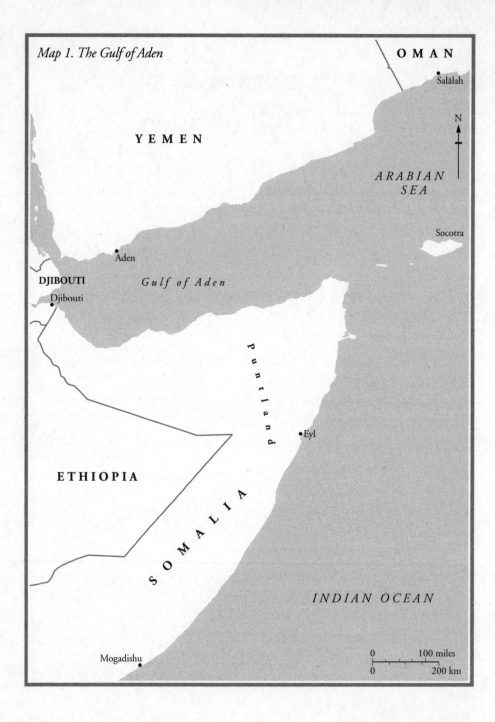

Map 1. The Gulf of Aden

OMAN

Salalah

YEMEN

N

ARABIAN SEA

Socotra

Aden

DJIBOUTI

Gulf of Aden

Djibouti

Puntland

Eyl

ETHIOPIA

S O M A L I A

INDIAN OCEAN

Mogadishu

| 0 | | 100 miles |
| 0 | | 200 km |

1. Them That Die'll Be the Lucky Ones . . .

Why pirates?

It is a good question, and one a lot of people asked me as I started to make preparations to investigate this dangerous world about which I knew almost nothing. I'd seen the newspaper reports, of course. I knew piracy was on the up. But I was also fresh out of Afghanistan. Over the previous couple of years I'd spent time in that dangerous war zone; I'd had Taliban snipers zeroing in on me, doing their best to kill me. I'd probably have been forgiven for taking it a bit easy.

Life doesn't work out like that, unfortunately. In January 2009 I was in Kajaki – one of the northern outposts of Helmand Province and scene of some of the fiercest fighting in Afghanistan. While I was there, a Marine by the name of Travis Mackin lost his life in an improvised explosive device strike near where I was accompanying his colleagues during an attack on a major Taliban stronghold. I suppose it goes without saying that I was impressed with the professionalism and tenacity of the Marines I met on that trip, and honoured to be accepted into their confidence. What I didn't know at the time was that in another part of the world the final act of a crime on the high seas was being played out, where the Royal Marines had been deployed in a very different conflict to that which the men at Kajaki were enduring. That crime was the hijacking of an oil tanker, the MV *Sirius Star*.

The *Sirius Star* is a big boat. A *very* big boat. It's classed as a VLCC – a very large crude carrier. You can say that again: well over 300 metres long, it can carry 2.2 million barrels of crude oil. How much that amount of black gold is worth depends on the value of oil, but even back then, with the world economy in free fall, the *Sirius Star*'s cargo would have been worth at least $100 million. As it set out from Saudi Arabia in November 2008, it was carrying about a quarter of that country's daily output of oil.

On 15 November 2008 the *Sirius Star* was heading south, 400 nautical miles from the coast of Kenya. Its destination: the United States. Its route: round the southern tip of Africa, past the Cape of Good Hope and then north-west across the Atlantic. It's easy to imagine that as the vessel passed through the waters off the eastern coast of Africa, its crew, while not being blasé, would at least have been reasonably confident of the ship's security. Sure, piracy was already a problem, but the incidents had generally taken place further north, in the Gulf of Aden. Moreover, ships of this size were generally safe. Surely just getting onto the boat would be nigh-on impossible. You'd need a brass neck, balls of steel and a very long ladder to attempt to hijack such a massive vessel. Wouldn't you?

If these were the thoughts of the *Sirius Star*'s owners and crew, they were mistaken. Because on that Saturday morning, at about 08.55, the boat was boarded by Somali pirates. They didn't mess around. By 09.02 the pirates had control of the bridge. The *Sirius Star* was so weighed down by its massive load of oil that its freeboard – the height between the deck and the waterline – was low. The crew, including two Britons, were taken hostage and the ship was

4

diverted from its original course, back up towards the Somali coastline. A couple of days later the pirates opened up communications with the ship's owners. They demanded a ransom of $25 million. The hijackers clearly knew the value of their haul, and were prepared to milk it for every last cent.

The eyes of the world were on the *Sirius Star*, but the hijackers held their nerve. They even released an audio tape to Al-Jazeera, the Middle Eastern news network. 'Negotiators are located on board the ship and on land. Once they have agreed on the ransom, it will be taken in cash to the oil tanker. We assure the safety of the ship that carries the ransom. We will mechanically count the money and we have machines that can detect fake money.' These pirates, then, were well organized and professional. They knew what they were doing.

The hostages were not mistreated. One of the Britons, Peter French, even managed to conduct an interview by phone. 'Our families don't have too much to worry about at the moment,' he said. 'Apart from the inconvenience of being locked up, our life is not too bad.' Nothing like a good British stiff upper lip. But if I were in his position, I imagine I'd be giving a great deal of thought to what would happen if the ransom *wasn't* paid. Would the pirates continue to be quite so considerate, or would they find a use for the automatic weapons they were carrying? As one of the pirates stated when they captured the vessel, 'We do not want long-term discussions to resolve the matter. The Saudis have ten days to comply, otherwise we will take action that could be disastrous.'

Disastrous for whom, I wonder . . .

The British government announced that there was no way they'd pay the ransom: giving in to hostage-taking was just an encouragement for people to do it again. The *Sirius Star*'s Saudi owners took a more pragmatic view. Not only were the 25 crew members their responsibility, they also had 100 million bucks to protect. And so the ransom negotiations started. They were long and drawn-out. On 25 November the pirates reduced their demand to $15 million. By January, it had come down even further. On 9 January 2009 the ship was released after the pirates received 3 million dollars. Sounds like a lot of money, but just think about what the shipowners had to lose . . .

A small plane dropped the ransom onto the deck of the *Sirius Star* by parachute. The pirates presumably checked the notes using the machines of which they had boasted, then they left the ship as swiftly as they had boarded it. The ending, however, was not a happy one for the Somali hijackers. Days after they left, their small boat apparently got into trouble in a storm. It capsized and five of the eight were drowned. A rumour later stated that the body of one was washed ashore with $150,000 in cash shoved into a plastic bag. What happened to the remaining three isn't clear. I guess they wouldn't be parading their presence any more than they had to – stepping into Somalia and announcing you have hundreds of thousands of dollars can't be good for your health. But I would later be told – totally unofficially, of course – that a team of private mercenaries had followed the hijackers, retrieved a large proportion of the money, capsized their boat and left the pirates for the fishes. Fact or rumour? Who knows . . .

The hijacking of the *Sirius Star* was significant for lots

of reasons. It was the first time such a big ship had been successfully pirated. It also marked an escalation in the pirates' field of operations – previously they had been confined to a much smaller area. The Somali pirates now roamed an area of about 1.1 million square miles, and there simply aren't enough military vessels in the world to patrol that amount of sea successfully.

I knew none of this in January 2009. I was busy with other worries, like how to avoid rocket-propelled grenade attacks from the local Taliban in Helmand Province – a very good way of keeping your mind occupied. But when the time came for me to say goodbye to 45 Victor Commando in Afghanistan and return home to London, it was clear that the piracy problem was current. It was happening now. There was no time for me to put my feet up. If I wanted to investigate pirates, to find out what was behind these attacks occurring in various hot spots and maybe even meet some of these people who were wreaking havoc and terror all round the world, the legwork would have to be done immediately.

And one thing was sure: the pirates weren't going to come to me. *I* was going to have to go to *them*.

All little boys want to be pirates. Why wouldn't they? The pirates of our imagination are romantic figures. They engage in acts of great daring. They seek out buried treasure and make their enemies walk the plank. If they're the Johnny Depp kind of pirate, they might even get the girl. And then they disappear, ready to plunder another day. The pirates we read about in books are villains, certainly. We know that. But, like highwaymen, perhaps we imagine that they're the acceptable face of villainy. That's why people don't mind their children dressing up with eyepatches and cutlasses.

I knew, of course, before I set out on my quest to track down some real-life pirates, that they aren't like that any more. That the pirates hijacking ships around the world armed with the kind of weaponry I'd previously seen in major war zones were not going to be of the yo-ho-ho-and-a-bottle-of-rum kind. But in fact they never *were* like that. Not in the real world. Successful pirates have always relied on the threat of force to achieve their ends, and the threat of force is only effective if people know you're willing to carry those threats out. Before I set off to learn about and meet modern-day pirates, I decided to learn something about the reality of their predecessors. Maybe if I knew something of the past, I'd learn something about the present. The stories I came across were unsettling, to say the least.

Our image of historical pirates is massively influenced by one book, huge in its time – a bestseller of the day. Robert Louis Stevenson's *Treasure Island* (1883), with its well-known anti-hero Long John Silver, is probably the most important source of all our ideas of what pirates used to be like, if not of the reality. The story of Jim Hawkins, the treasure map and Long John Silver's piratical mutiny aboard the *Hispaniola* is probably the most famous pirate story of all time. It's thanks to this book that we think of treasure maps, parrots, wooden legs and desert islands; it's thanks to this book that little boys grow up under the misapprehension that X always marks the spot . . . As with many writers, Robert Louis Stevenson allowed himself plenty of licence in the story's telling. Real-life pirates were no more disposed to search for chests of buried treasure than anyone else – in fact they would steal whatever they could get their hands on, and their loot was as likely to be made up of cargos of rope or sugar as it was pieces of eight and gold doubloons.

That said, Stevenson knew what he was talking about, and we can learn a lot about the real pirates of the day by reading his story. Take Long John Silver, the ship's cook with a wooden leg. It was commonplace for old sailors and those who had been wounded at sea to join expeditions as the ship's cook, a role that required a working knowledge of the vessel if not the physical ability to sail it. And for a sailor to be wounded – even to lose a limb – was a pretty regular occurrence. There are plenty of examples of pirates losing arms and legs during skirmishes at sea. Perhaps the most eye-watering is that of a man called William Phillips. He sustained a bad wound to his left leg during a fight between two pirate ships. Unfortunately there was no doctor or surgeon on board. There was, however, a carpenter, and it was decided that he was the man for the job. He used his largest saw to cut William Phillips' leg from his body – history doesn't record how long it took, or what sort of inhuman noises the patient made as the saw's teeth cut through his gristle and bone. We do know, however, that once the leg was removed, the carpenter heated his axe in a flame and used the flat side of it to cauterize the bleeding stump. He burned off more flesh than he intended, but somehow William Phillips survived the operation. When Long John Silver promised, 'Them that die'll be the lucky ones,' perhaps the tortures he had in mind were derived from the day he lost *his* leg.

Silver's parrot, Cap'n Flint, is almost as famous as he is, and while the idea of a talking bird on his shoulder sounds fanciful, sailors regularly brought back exotic birds and other animals from their trips abroad. Parrots, it seems, were especially popular, not only because they were colourful and could be taught how to speak, but also because they were a low-maintenance pet on board ship.

And of course *Treasure Island* is the archetypal story of an inside job. When I conducted my investigation into modern-day piracy, I learned that while many aspects of the story might belong to another age, Long John Silver's modus operandi is very much alive and well.

Piracy, however, has been around for a lot longer than *Treasure Island*. Ancient Greek mosaics show images of ships being attacked by pirates, and the Vikings were a piratical nation. The pirates that spark our imagination the most, however, arrived in the seventeenth and eighteenth centuries, and they were a rum bunch. Take Edward 'Ned' Low. He was a real-life pirate of the Caribbean, and a man with a reputation. He was born in London in 1690 in abject poverty. His family were thieves and pickpockets, and he soon fell into the family business. At the age of about 30, however, Low decided on a career change, joining a sloop – a one-masted sailing boat – bound for Honduras. Low worked honestly as a rigger on that first voyage, but he didn't stay honest for long. When the captain of the ship told him one day that he would have to wait for his food, Low took exception. He picked up a loaded musket and fired it, missing the captain but shooting a shipmate through the throat. Messy.

Low and his friends – unsurprisingly – were kicked off the boat, and it was then that they turned pirate, taking over another sloop off Rhode Island. It was a short career, but a brutal one. He became noted for his acts of viciousness and torture. On one occasion, when the captain of a Portuguese ship allowed a substantial quantity of money to fall into the sea rather than let it be stolen, Low cut off the man's lips with his cutlass, fried them in front of him then forced him to eat them while they were still hot. For pudding, he murdered the entire crew.

It's said that Low once announced that one of his victims was 'a greasy fellow, who would fry well'. To prove his point, he burned him alive. One of Low's crew later wrote of his time under the pirate's command. 'Of all the piratical crews that were ever heard of, none of the English name came up to this in barbarity. Their mirth and their anger had much the same effect, for both were usually gratified with the cries and groans of their prisoners; so that they almost as often murdered a man from the excess of good humour as out of passion and resentment; and the unfortunate could never be assured of safety from them, for danger lurked in their very smiles.' All in all, he made Captain Hook look like a pussycat.

Ned Low was one of the better-known pirates to emerge from what has been dubbed the Golden Age of Piracy, a period that spanned the 1650s to the 1720s. There were many others, some of whose names have passed into myth. Edward Teach was more commonly known as Blackbeard. Teach was born in Bristol, took to the seas at an early age and spent the first part of his career on privateers. These were armed ships which had permission – recognized by international law – to attack the ships of an enemy nation. A proportion of the loot was handed over to the crown; the rest was kept by the privateers. Originally, privateer licences were intended to allow ships to recoup any losses they sustained as a result of attack by enemy vessels; in time, though, they became a cheap way of boosting a country's naval forces. Perhaps the most famous privateer was Sir Francis Drake, who during the sixteenth century was the scourge of Spanish shipping. He shared his booty with Elizabeth I, and received a knighthood for his efforts. Privateers could not be arrested for piracy, but in practice many of them were simply official pirates. And it was not beyond the scruples of many of them to turn their hand to acts of genuine piracy.

Teach was a privateer during England's ongoing war with Spain, targeting Spanish ships, but when Britain withdrew from the war, many privateers turned pirate. Teach was among them. He drew his nickname, of course, from his enormous black beard, which he decorated with ribbons and slung over his ears. Traditional pictures of Blackbeard show him carrying several pistols hanging from his clothes – not entirely fanciful as the weapons of the day were unreliable, especially if they got wet, which was an occupational hazard. In Blackbeard's line of work, you really wanted to make sure you had a backup if that happened. You wanted, quite literally, to keep your powder dry.

Blackbeard's reputation was fearsome, and rumours of his barbarity travelled far. It was said that he once shot his first mate just to remind the crew of his position, and that he would allow his fourteenth (yes, fourteenth) wife to be raped by up to six members of his crew in a single night – once he had had his own way with her. In fact, although he was, financially speaking, a very successful pirate, there is little actual evidence of all this barbarity. The same can't be said for his somewhat gruesome death. A price was put on Blackbeard's head and he was hunted down by a Lieutenant Maynard. They fought with swords and pistols, and it took Maynard five bullets and twenty slashes with a sword to kill the pirate. Either Maynard's weapons were dodgy, or Blackbeard was a hard bastard. Once he was dead, his head was cut off and hung from the side of Maynard's ship – a reminder to anyone who saw it what fate pirates could expect if they were brought to justice.

Ned Low and Blackbeard were buccaneers – pirates who operated around the Caribbean and off the coast of South America. Nowadays 'buccaneer' has connotations of swashbuckling romance. The original buccaneers were actually French settlers on the Caribbean island of Hispaniola (now split into Haiti and the Dominican Republic). They looked after herds of livestock and for food used to smoke strips of meat over open fires. The French word for this method of cooking is *boucaner*, and these herders were a pretty wild and unsavoury bunch. When they realized there was a better living to be made pirating the Spanish galleons returning home laden with treasures from Mexico and South America, they lost their enthusiasm for livestock farming, underwent a quick career change and the original buccaneers were born.

Some buccaneers were privateers; others were out-and-out pirates. In many cases, the distinction between the two became a bit hazy. Sometimes they joined forces and attacked entire cities. Even those on the more criminal side, however, lived a weirdly democratic existence. Plunder was shared out according to an established system, and a ship's captain could be voted out by his crew – a novel way of doing things in the seventeenth century. Perhaps that was why, even back then, stories of buccaneers became popular with landlubbers.

Life on pirate ships was no cosy utopia, however. Rules were strict, and if you broke them you were flogged or killed. Any pirate found stealing from his shipmates or deserting during battle would be marooned on a desert island – a slow and agonizing way to meet your death. An extremely popular book at the time, written by a Dutchman called Alexander Exquemelin, was called *The Buccaneers of America*. Exquemelin knew what he was talking about because he spent 12 years travelling on buccaneer ships as a surgeon. His book had a pretty colourful cast of characters, such as the French buccaneer Francis L'Ollonais. 'It was the custom of L'Ollonais,' he tells us, 'that, having tormented any persons and they not confessing, he would instantly cut them in pieces with his anger, and pull out their tongues.' On one occasion, when L'Ollonais wanted to gain entry to a Caribbean town, some Spanish soldiers made an unsuccessful attempt at ambushing him. The buccaneer captured the ambushers and forced them to tell him how to get into the town without being seen. According to Exquemelin, 'he drew his cutlass, and with it cut open the breast of one of those poor Spaniards, and pulling out his heart with his sacrilegious hands, began to bite and gnaw it with his teeth, like a ravenous wolf, saying to the rest: I will serve you all alike, if you show me not another way.'

L'Ollonais wasn't the only one with a penchant for torture. A Dutch buccaneer called Roche Brasiliano derived his kicks from getting blind drunk and roasting Spanish prisoners alive over a spit. Whatever turns you on . . .

The Caribbean provided rich pickings for the buccaneers because of the trade routes that took a huge amount of commercial shipping to that part of the world. Merchant boats would load up in Europe with manufactured goods and weapons, then sail to Africa, where they would trade these goods for slaves. The slaves would then be taken to the Caribbean to be exchanged for commodities such as sugar, tobacco and cocoa, and the ships would return to Europe. This triangular trade route, however, was not the only one, and the buccaneers of the Caribbean were not the only pirates. The Mediterranean also played host to them, and those pirates that operated there were known as corsairs. There were some European corsairs, but they were far outnumbered by those from the northern coast of Africa, operating especially from Tunis, Tripoli, Algiers and Salé. This was known by Europeans as the Barbary Coast. The pirates that originated from these ports were known as the Barbary corsairs.

The Barbary corsairs terrorized the Mediterranean, the West African coast and the North Atlantic long before the so-called Golden Age of Piracy. As early as the eleventh century, when the Christian countries of Europe were waging war on Islam and other faiths in the Crusades, many Barbary pirates were given permission by the rulers of Muslim North Africa to attack European ships. The effect of these pirates was massive. They wouldn't just attack ships, but also coastal towns. Huge lengths of the Spanish and Italian coasts remained unoccupied for hundreds of years because of the piracy threat. In 1631 almost all the inhabitants of a town on the south coast of Ireland were captured by pirates and taken to the Barbary coast, where an unpleasant fate awaited them. Between 1580 and 1680, around 850,000 European captives of the Barbary pirates were sold into slavery in North Africa. White slaves in North Africa were not nearly as numerous as black slaves elsewhere – nothing like – but thanks to the Barbary corsairs there were still a hell of a lot of them.

The Barbary pirates kept a proportion of their slaves for themselves, and the lives of these unfortunate captives could be miserable, especially if – as often happened – they were used to row the pirates' galleys, the light winds of the Mediterranean being less suited to sailing ships. This was brutal work. The slaves were chained to their oars, and anyone not pulling their weight was whipped. Many died from exhaustion or went mad. If it became clear that they were no longer any use, it didn't take long to throw them over the side (the idea that pirates forced people to walk the plank is just a myth – these brutal men had no patience for such ceremonial methods). The slaves ate where they were chained, they slept where they were chained, they even went to the toilet where they were chained. An Englishman called Francis Knight wrote of his stint as a galley slave in the early seventeenth century, 'The stroke regular and punctual, their heads shaved unto the skull, their faces disfigured with disbarbing, their bodies all naked, only a short linen pair of breeches to cover their privities . . . all their bodies pearled with a bloody sweat.' In around 1670, the families of some of these captives wrote an appeal to the House of Commons: 'The [slave owners] do frequently bugger the said captives, or . . . run iron into their fundaments, rip open their bellies with knives, cut their britches across, and washing them with vinegar and salt, and hot oil, draw them in carts like horses.'

Some slaves were consigned to a life of rowing for decades without ever leaving their ships. Others would return to land during the winter months, when it was too treacherous for the Barbary pirates to be on the high seas. Here they were set to work building harbour walls or constructing new ships. They were given very little to eat or drink, and if they collapsed their masters would beat them until they got up again. They were given a change of clothes once a year.

The Barbary pirates didn't limit themselves to taking men. Christian women were fair game too. They were sold to the rulers of the Barbary coast and became part of their harems. If they were lucky, they'd be engaged only as harem attendants on the off chance that they might attract a ransom. Male slaves could also be bought out of slavery through payment of a ransom. But most of them came from poor backgrounds, so this rarely happened – unless they were the lucky recipients of money from charities back home set up for this purpose.

The most famous of the Barbary corsairs were two brothers who went by the name of Barbarossa, though only one of them – Aroudj – had the red beard from which they derived their name. His brother Hayreddin, however, became the more famous seaman, and in later years he died his beard red with henna out of respect for his brother. The Barbarossas came from the Ottoman empire, and Hayreddin was a hugely successful privateer around the Mediterranean. But he was more than that. He became admiral in chief of the Ottoman sultan's fleet, and thanks to his exploits the empire controlled the Mediterranean for many years. Barbarossa was a national hero – in modern-day Istanbul there is a boulevard named after him.

Another well-known Barbary corsair happened, peculiarly, to be an Englishman. His name was John Ward and he spent his early career as a privateer for Queen Elizabeth, plundering Spanish ships under licence from her. When Elizabeth died and James came to the throne, he ended the war with Spain. Ward, like many privateers, was put out of business. And so he turned pirate. Having stolen an enormous 32-gun warship, he spent two years terrorizing merchant shipping around the Mediterranean. In about 1606 he arranged with the ruler of Tunisia to use Tunis as a base in return for a proportion of his spoils. He converted to Islam and changed his name to Yusuf Reis. Ward's actions made him ever so slightly unpopular in his home country. One contemporary report described him as being 'very short with little hair, and that quite white, bald in front; swarthy face and beard. Speaks little and almost always swearing. Drunk from morn till night . . . the habits of a thorough salt. A fool and an idiot out of his trade.' The English ambassador to Venice called him 'the greatest scoundrel that ever sailed from England' – and in a country that wasn't short on pirates, he was up against some pretty stiff competition. Still, he lived out the rest of his life in Tunis, and died a rich man.

The Western powers were ready to condemn the action of these Muslim corsairs, but they weren't exactly lily-white themselves. There were Christian corsairs too, who targeted North African shipping. The Knights of St John, for example, were based in Malta and regularly hit Muslim vessels – so much so that in 1720 there were around 10,000 Muslim slaves in Malta alone. Many Mediterranean galleys were manned by Muslim slaves, and while it was true that there were an eye-watering number of white slaves in North Africa at the time, it was by no means a one-sided evil. In 1714 a British naval officer wrote that 'amongst the several towns situated on the coast of Spain, there may be moors purchased at very reasonable rates, such as are aged, blind or lame. It's no matter, all will pass so they have life.' A charming sentiment, and not an infrequent one in those sad days of slavery. As is always the case, every coin has two sides.

But the Barbary pirates were a major risk to Western shipping. In order to minimize the risk, France and other countries started paying bribes – they called them tributes – to the Barbary states. These tributes took the form of gold, jewels and other goods, and meant that the attentions of the corsairs were directed towards the weaker powers of Europe and, after the American War of Independence, the United States (until independence American ships had been under the protection of the mighty Royal Navy). In 1800, 20 per cent of the American government's annual spending was on ransoms to the Barbary corsairs, and it was this that caused the fledgling United States to build its first navy and engage the Barbary nations in the First and Second Barbary Wars – the US's first, but often forgotten, brush with Islamic nations. The newly formed United States Marines fought in these wars, and wore thick leather collars to protect them from the cutlass swipes of the corsairs. To this day, US Marines are known as leathernecks. (Interestingly, Royal Marines are sometimes called bootnecks because they would wrap their leather gaiters around their necks to stop themselves being slashed by mutinous crews.)

Despite this anti-piracy effort, it was not until 1816 that the threat of the Barbary corsairs was eliminated. The British navy achieved this by crushing the might of Algiers, killing about 8,000 men and destroying every building in the city. A British warship would not be called upon to fight the threat of piracy for another two centuries. When that happened, it would have the dubious honour of carrying me on board . . .

The real world of pirates, then, was a brutal one. Unlike the pirates of fiction, who are often portrayed as roguish adventurers, the pirates of history were hard, mean men. Violence and cruelty were second nature to them and their lives were tough and dangerous: for every John Ward who ended his days a rich man, there were many more Ned Lows and Blackbeards, gruesomely beheaded or hanged for their crimes after only a couple of years of plundering on the high seas.

In short, encountering pirates was one of the most frightening things that could happen at sea. They were heavily armed, determined and, surrounded by mile upon mile of water, there was nowhere the victims could go to escape them.

Many things have changed since those days. But some things haven't. Seventy per cent of the earth's surface is covered with water. Ninety per cent of all goods are transported by sea. Just look around your house. Tea bags? They came here by boat. Sugar? By boat. Ikea furniture? By boat. The clothes on your back and the car on your driveway? You guessed it. As has been the case for hundreds and hundreds of years, from the days of the Greek pirates, through the Golden Age of Piracy, where there's trade, there's crime. And just like in the days of Ned Low and Blackbeard, coming under attack in the middle of the ocean is not like coming under attack on land, because there's nowhere to run and there are no police stations out at sea.

Modern-day pirates, I realized as I prepared to go out and find them, were not so different from the pirates of history. They were ruthless. They were daring. They were heavily armed – not with cutlasses and pistols but with automatic weapons and rocket-propelled grenades. And if my experiences in the past had taught me nothing else, they had taught me this: when someone is carrying that kind of weaponry, chances are they're prepared to use it . . .

2. Pirate Alley

On 6 January 2009, just as the hijacking of the *Sirius Star* was coming to an end and while I was still in Kajaki, a 44-year-old Somali man by the name of Ibrahim Hussein Duale was going about his business, monitoring a school in the Gedo region of Somalia, near the Kenyan and Ethiopian borders. Duale worked for an organization called the World Food Programme. His role was to monitor the feeding of the schoolchildren in this ravaged country. A worthwhile occupation, I'd say. A good man.

Three masked gunmen entered the school. Duale happened to be sitting down at the time. The gunmen told him to get to his feet. He obeyed. And then, without explanation or hesitation, the gunmen shot him dead. Duale had a wife and five children, and was the third World Food Programme staff member to be killed in three months. Two days later, the total went up to four.

A shocking story. But where Ibrahim Hussein Duale came from, crimes like this are commonplace. In a weird kind of way, they're not even crimes. Somalia has no functioning government. Lawlessness is the norm. I've been to some tough places in the world, but the thought of going there made me a bit green around the gills. And the more I learned about that troubled place, the more nervous I became.

The modern history of the country we now think of as Somalia, like the history of most African countries, is deeply complicated. In the late nineteenth century a number of European powers attempted to establish themselves in the area. One look at the map is enough to understand why. The country's northern coastline is along the Gulf of Aden. If you want to transport goods from the Middle East up through the Red Sea and along the Suez Canal to the Mediterranean, your route has to take you through the Gulf of Aden – unless you want the expense of sailing south around the tip of Africa. To control the ports along the Somali coast would be to have a great economic advantage.

The British made treaties with a number of Somali chiefs, guaranteeing them security in return for establishing the protectorate of British Somaliland. The protectorate was bordered on three sides by Ethiopia, French Somaliland and Italian Somaliland, and covered the area around the northern coast. The colonialists were not universally popular. In fact, that's a bit of an understatement: between 1899 and 1920, British Somaliland came under regular, brutal attack from the forces of a religious leader called Sayyid Muhammad Abdullah Hassan. A bit of a mouthful – no wonder the British nicknamed him the Mad Mullah. Hassan was eventually suppressed, but 20 years later things were shaken up again with the arrival of the Second World War, when for a short while the Italians took British Somaliland. It was reconquered a few months later.

In 1960 British Somaliland gained independence and unified with Italian Somaliland to form the Somali Republic. What followed was the internal strife common to many post-colonial African states, culminating in a devastating civil war that started in 1991. The repressive Siad Barré fell from power, sparking a spiral of revolution and counter-revolution as some factions tried to reinstate him and others did whatever they thought necessary to stop this happening. The result was total anarchy. The northern region of Somaliland declared itself independent of the rest of the country, but the international community refused to recognize it.

The humanitarian situation became dire. Fighting raged between warlords, starting in the capital Mogadishu but soon spreading throughout the country; in the meantime, the ordinary people starved. From all over the world, governments sent food aid to help the starving. It's estimated, however, that the warlords stole 80 per cent of the food that reached Somalia and sold it to other countries in order to raise money for weapons. And so both the starvation and the violence worsened. By the end of 1992, approximately 500,000 Somalis were prematurely dead and 1.5 million displaced.

The UN approved the insertion of a United States-led peacekeeping force. It was called Operation Restore Hope. If only. Anyone who has seen the movie *Black Hawk Down* will know something of the Battle of Mogadishu. A force of approximately 160 American soldiers, with 19 aircraft and 12 vehicles, was dispatched to capture a high-ranking accomplice of one of the warlords on the outskirts of the capital. A lot of muscle to pick up one guy. During the operation, however, militants shot down two Black Hawk helicopters with rocket-propelled grenades. A number of wounded American soldiers were trapped at the crash site and came under attack during the night in a fierce firefight on the streets of Mogadishu. A task force was dispatched the next day to rescue them, but the casualties had been high: 19 American soldiers and more than 1,000 Somali militia dead.

The Battle of Mogadishu was a bloodbath, and it blunted the Americans' appetite for involvement in Somalia. By 1995, all UN personnel had been withdrawn from the region, but Somalia was as volatile as ever, and its people were suffering just as badly.

Fast-forward to now. After years of internal strife there is a transitional government of sorts, backed by Ethiopian troops, but it has very little in the way of actual authority. Most of the country is a violent mess and, as ever, it is the ordinary people who suffer the most. Killing, looting and gang rape are rife, instigated both by insurgent and government forces. One Amnesty International report tells of a 17-year-old girl being raped by Ethiopian troops. When her two brothers – aged 13 and 14 – tried to intervene, the soldiers gouged out their eyes with bayonets. Others tell of men having their testicles removed, and of people having their throats cut and being left to die in the street. They even have their own word for this method of slaughter, which roughly translates as 'to kill like a goat'. Without a proper functioning government, nobody is held accountable for these crimes. And nobody stops them.

The dire situation in Somalia is made even more difficult – and probably unsolvable – by the complicated system of clan loyalties and family groupings that exists there. Somalis themselves barely understand these loyalties; for a foreigner they're almost impossible. The most prominent clans are the Hawiye, the Darod, the Ishaak and the Rahanwein, but within each clan there is a fiendish network of sub-clans with complex hierarchies and impenetrable webs of loyalties.

The clan system has been an essential part of Somali politics for as long as anyone can remember. Any new leader will ensure all the plum jobs go to members of his own clan at the expense of others while inter-clan rivalries and arguments are constantly escalating into violence. Moreover, one of the characteristics of the clan system is the payment of any earnings to those further up the hierarchy of your clan – a kind of African Cosa Nostra.

The result is a country ripped apart. Around 3.25 million people are in need of humanitarian assistance in Somalia – that's about a third of the population. One in six children under the age of five suffers acute malnourishment; one in four dies before this age. Life expectancy at birth is 42. So if I lived there, I'd probably be dead. (Don't say it.)

The World Food Programme provides food aid to more than 2 million people a month. That's a lot of food. It's got to get there somehow. Like almost everything else in the world, most of the WFP's supplies arrive in Somalia by sea. Ninety per cent, to be precise. But cargo ships are increasingly reluctant to make the dangerous voyage to the coast of Somalia. Why? Because just as the staff of the WFP – men like Ibrahim Hussein Duale – are not immune from the danger and unpredictability of the region, so their ships are not immune from the country's other great problem.

And that problem, as you might have guessed, is the pirates.

Piracy is not new in the Gulf of Aden. It's not for nothing, then, that sailors have nicknamed it Pirate Alley. The reason pirates, historically, have been drawn to this waterway is the same reason the colonialists were drawn to it centuries ago: it forms a vital passage for trade. Each year 23,000 vessels pass through this waterway. And where there are trade ships, there's money to be made – legally or illegally.

Off the coastline of Somalia lies the island of Socotra. Socotra falls under Yemeni jurisdiction, but in many ways it is its own place. A UNESCO natural world heritage site, Socotra has an amazing abundance of plant life. It is one of the few places in the world where you'll find the dragon's blood tree, whose bright red sap was once thought of as a powerful medicine and became a valuable commodity. In addition, Socotra was always rich in frankincense, myrrh and aloe. During the first century AD these commodities made Socotra an important staging post and a destination for ships from all over the world.

Times changed. Global demand for frankincense and myrrh reduced; better medicines than dragon's blood came along. Between the tenth and fourteenth centuries the beautiful island of Socotra, situated as it was in the centre of an important trade route, became notorious as a haven for pirates instead. From here they could run riot across the Indian Ocean and even up the Red Sea. Merchant ships often had to resort to the use of an ancient incendiary weapon known as Greek fire to keep them away. Greek fire was a mixture of chemicals that could be sprayed, burning, towards nearby ships, with the advantage that it continued to burn even on water. Really not what you want when your boat is made of wood.

In 1507 Socotra was colonized by the Portuguese, followed by the British in the nineteenth century. At the start of the Second World War an RAF airfield was built, and following British withdrawal there were rumours that the Soviet Union maintained a naval base there. Nowadays its reputation as a pirate haven is firmly part of its history, but the Gulf of Aden hasn't stopped being very important to a lot of people, and the pirates have found other havens on the Somali coastline from which to operate. Somalia, with its lack of anything remotely resembling law and order, is an obvious choice. Recently, the number of recorded pirate attacks has gone up dramatically. In 2004 there were five; in the first nine months of 2008 there were more than sixty. In 2008 Somali pirates raised an estimated $30 million in ransoms. Insurance premiums for cargo ships travelling through the Gulf of Aden have increased ten-fold.

When my team and I make a documentary film, there's a lot of work that goes on behind the scenes. We are given safety briefings and have to commission detailed risk assessments (I do sometimes wonder if I must be a risk assessor's worst nightmare). We try to find local fixers in the countries to which we're travelling, people with a knowledge of the area and a book of contacts that will help grease the wheels and make the shoot run smoothly and – with a bit of luck – safely. The process has served us well. It's got us into some dangerous parts of dangerous countries, and facilitated interviews with dangerous men. It's allowed us to meet paramilitaries in Colombia who'd kill you without a second thought; it's taken us into slums as far apart as Rio and Kenya where you run a very real risk of having your throat cut for a handful of coins; it's taken us into the most dangerous war zone in the world.

Somalia, though, was a different matter. We were told that if we so much as set foot on Somali soil, we would be killed or kidnapped.

Not might. *Would*. All the journalists to have set foot outside the port of Mogadishu in recent years have been shot.

This point of view was reinforced when I went to meet a guy in London who freelances for MI6, the CIA and other intelligence agencies. His job title? Special Operations Operative. To you and me, he's a spook, and I can't reveal his name or anything else about him. His work regularly takes him into Somalia, and as we sat down to chat I asked him what it was, exactly, that he did for a living.

'I fix problems,' he told me.

What sort of problems?

'Pretty much anything. It could be issues between tribes, issues between certain persons, political issues . . .' He didn't seem too keen to elaborate, and I didn't push it.

I asked the spook what it was like to walk down the street in Mogadishu.

'It can have its moments.' He explained that there is a standing kill order against Caucasian people in Somalia, and I asked him exactly what that meant. 'A kill order is where different tribes, different groups or different factions decide they're not going to allow certain people or an individual into an area. Word will spread on the streets that if this person, or type of person, is seen, then get rid of them. It might be that they take them and throw them in the back of a van somewhere, or it could be quite simply that they open fire.'

But surely if you're with the right people . . .

'The problem with somewhere like Somalia is that there's no right people. You can be on one side of the fence and the other side will always be after you. You take your chances. It's 50-50 either way.'

Was the spook armed when he walked around the streets of Somalia?

'Most definitely.'

And did he have close protection?

'No. The more people you have, the more chance there is of drawing attention to yourself.'

I asked what I thought might sound like a ridiculous question, but he didn't seem to think it was ridiculous at all: did he wear a disguise?

He nodded. 'Depends on where I am, but yes, I can wear a disguise.'

I wondered if our man had ever had a kill order placed specifically on him. He looked a bit uncomfortable. 'There's been people that have been unhappy with me,' he conceded.

From everything I'd learned about Somalia, I was intrigued to know how he got into the country – presumably he didn't just turn up at the airport with his suitcase and passport. He explained that the methods of entry varied: a four-by-four across the border, small planes or a small boat across from Yemen. So how difficult would it be, I wondered, for myself and a camera team to get onto the mainland?

'Getting there,' the spook explained, 'is not your hardest or biggest problem. It's what's going to happen when you're there. Word would spread quickly – a film crew turns up with a famous presenter. There's a good chance you could become another asset. At the same time there's a good chance you could upset a few severe people and you'll never leave the place.'

I could tell by the look on his face and the sound of his voice that he wasn't exaggerating. 'Because of the work you do,' I said, 'you travel to a lot of dangerous places. How would you rate this on a scale of one to ten?'

'It's certainly up there as one of the worst places in the world at this moment in time.'

Our spook knew his onions, and I was more than happy to believe everything he told me about Somalia. More to the point, his information was backed up by the other investigations we undertook. There was no chance of the camera team and me getting any kind of insurance to go there, and no matter how hard we tried, we couldn't find a fixer willing to set things up for us – not for any money. We tried to arrange to join a World Food Programme ship taking food aid into Mogadishu. Nothing doing. If we set foot on land, it was explained to us, we'd be shot. Everyone said the same thing: risk going there and we'd barely last a few hours. No matter who we asked, the reply was identical: stay away. Somalia is just too damn dangerous.

It was clear that we couldn't even think about venturing into Somalia and I had mixed feelings about that. Half of me was disappointed: I knew that searching for a Somali pirate out at sea would not be straightforward. Unlike some of the gang members I'd met in the past, who often had a drum to bang or just liked the idea of being on TV, these guys would have absolutely no reason to talk to me and would be distinctly camera shy. The other half of me – the more sensible side, I suppose – couldn't help thinking, Thank fuck for that. I'd had a pretty exciting couple of years, got myself into some hairy situations, and I didn't fancy rounding them off by becoming another dismal statistic of the Somali civil war.

However, instead of setting foot on Somali soil, if we

31

were to track down some pirates there was no getting away from the fact that we'd need to spend a good deal of time in Somali waters, and that, as anyone who had been reading or listening to the news over the past couple of months knew, would be no picnic. It was some comfort that when the *Sirius Star* had been taken, the pirates had chosen not to mistreat their prisoners, but we all knew that hostage situations could have a very different outcome. Somali pirates were armed, dangerous and desperate. It's not a good combination.

Dangerous it might be, but if I was going to meet any pirates it was clear that I couldn't avoid these waters. Our investigation did not start there, however. It started in London, at the sleek offices of the International Maritime Bureau – ironically just metres from the former site of Execution Dock, where pirates, smugglers and mutineers were hanged. Their bodies were not removed from the gallows when they were dead; rather they were left swinging there until the tide of the Thames had covered their heads three times. The corpses of the worst criminals were then tarred to preserve them and taken to Graves Point at the mouth of the Thames. Here they were gibbeted – strung up – as a warning to other sailors of what might happen if they were tempted by a life of piracy. (One of history's most famous pirates, Captain Kidd, had his body displayed there for three years.)

Attitudes have changed somewhat in the couple of hundred years since Execution Dock was abolished in 1830. The IMB is a non-profit-making organization whose role is to combat maritime fraud and suppress piracy. They've got their work cut out. The IMB has links with

Interpol and was instrumental in the creation of the IMB Piracy Reporting Centre in Kuala Lumpur. Before this organization was established in 1992, ships that had been hit by pirates had nowhere to turn as more often than not local law-enforcement agencies would simply ignore the fact that they even had a problem with piracy. Now, acts of piracy can be described to the Reporting Centre, and the result is an ongoing live database of incidents that warns shipping exactly where the current hot spots are. Anyone can read it on the Internet, and it's a pretty eye-opening source of information.

At the IMB's headquarters I met Captain Mukundun, a mild-mannered but no-nonsense former sailor. I asked him if he had any idea how many pirates were currently operating in the Gulf of Aden. The figures were as bad as I expected. 'We are told,' Mukundun said, 'that there are many hundreds of young Somalis seeking a career in piracy. It's one of the most sought-after careers in a country where there is no proper economy.'

I wanted to know, from the mouth of an expert, how violent these pirates were. Mukundun explained to me that they were very well armed with automatic weapons and rocket-propelled grenade launchers (like I hadn't seen enough of those over the past few months). 'In trying to board the ships,' the captain said, 'they will use as much violence as they can.'

Captain Mukundun's words really brought it home to me that while this trip might not present the more immediate dangers of Helmand Province, it still had the potential to be perilous. And where most people who travel through the area go out of their way to *avoid* pirates, we intended to do the very opposite: to seek out these dangerous, unpredictable and often desperate individuals. If we were going to spend time around the Gulf of Aden, we would have to take some pretty serious precautions.

For my previous travels I had been on what are known as Hostile Environment Courses. Generally run by experienced former members of the military, these courses teach you techniques that to some people might sound like common sense, but which you'd be glad you knew if you found yourself in trouble. They teach you what to do if your vehicle finds itself in a minefield. (Answer: get out of the back of the vehicle and walk away along the tracks that it's made. That way, you know you're not going to step on a pressure plate.) They teach you how to ascertain who has the most serious injuries if your car is involved in a crash. (Answer: check the pulses and breathing of the injured passengers.) They teach you whether or not to move a seriously injured person. (Answer: only if their life is going to be put at greater risk if you don't. If you can keep them still, do. You really don't want to move someone with, say, a punctured lung if you can help it, but if there are bullets flying through the windscreen and he's going to get hit in the head, get him the hell out of there.) They teach you how to make a makeshift neck brace out of a shirt or jacket, and how to make a tourniquet if someone is losing blood at a ferocious rate. They teach you how to identify anti-personnel mines and where the best place is to take cover; they give you the low-down on some common weapons and show you how they work. And the most important thing they teach you? The closer you get to the front, the more chance you have of getting shot . . .

Like I say, all useful stuff in its way, and of course I'd spent time in a highly hostile land environment anyway, which teaches you more than you can ever learn from any training course. But being at sea is different from being in the desert. Not necessarily more dangerous, but different. There might not be any anti-personnel mines in the Gulf of Aden; but equally it's difficult to take cover when you're surrounded by miles of open ocean. We could take certain precautions – each member of the crew was issued with a tracking device, for example, and a means of alerting London if we ran into trouble – but our first trip in search of pirates still had the potential to be a very hazardous operation. If the pirates were willing to board a vessel the size of the *Sirius Star*, just where would they stop? What we needed was a bit of protection. A bit of muscle. We wanted to be on board a boat that even the pirates of Somalia wouldn't consider raiding.

And that was where HMS *Northumberland* came in.

3. Action Stations

I wouldn't be the first member of the family to step on board a Royal Navy warship. I could only hope, however, that I wouldn't have the maritime luck of some of my fore-bears.

I come from a family of seafarers. My mum's grandfather was known to everyone – including my mum – as Pop. That was short for Popeye the Sailor Man. In the little village in Norfolk where he lived the final years of his life he was the only man to have gone to sea. He joined the merchant navy at the age of 12, and spent the last 17 years of his career, up to the age of 72, as a quartermaster on a pleasure cruiser called the *Andes*. (A quartermaster at sea is different from an army quartermaster. In the British merchant navy this was the person who actually steered the ship, and was so called because the duty was divided into four shifts. On pirate ships during the Golden Age of Piracy the quarter-master ranked just below the captain, and could even veto the captain's decisions under certain circumstances. I'm pleased to report, though, that Pop kept entirely to the straight and narrow during his long years at sea.)

Pop was shipwrecked several times, but survived them all. On one of these occasions he was marooned on a Pacific Island with members of the United States navy. He was missing for several months, eventually turning up on his home doorstep in a US uniform. During his time at sea he was involved in the transportation of troops all over the world. He watched the bombing of the Suez Canal, just north of the Gulf of Aden; he took troops to Korea; and during the Second World War he was involved in the 'Russian run', taking supplies out to the Russian troops. My mum still remembers him bringing her back a pair of fur-lined leather Russian boots. They must have seemed very exotic to a little girl all those decades ago . . .

Pop's brothers were also naval men. Two of them jumped ship in Canada, which was a serious offence – they had to wait for the monarch to die and the resulting amnesty to be declared before they could even write back to their families. A third brother was a submariner. He died just after the First World War from brain damage, probably caused by lack of oxygen in the submarines. He left four children, two of whom – Arthur Buck and his younger brother Bertie – joined the navy at the start of the Second World War. They were posted to HMS *Hood* – an Admiral-class battle-cruiser, the largest warship the British possessed and the pride of the Royal Navy.

This was early in the war, and Britain was in a precarious situation. France – her closest ally – had fallen, and although the Americans had been helping out with weapons and other supplies, they were still months away from entering the fray. As an island nation, Britain relied heavily on foreign imports to keep going and the only way these imports could arrive was by sea. The German navy – the Kriegsmarine – pulled out all the stops to ensure that these goods never made it. And the best way for them to do that was through the use of their submarines, or U-boats. The U-boats did their work with ruthless efficiency. Between September 1939 and May 1941 they sank something in the region of 3 million tonnes of shipping and it hit the country hard.

Hitler had realized for a long time that sea assets were essential in a war against Britain and ordered the construction of a modern fleet made up of a new type of ship. To this end the Germans launched the famous battleship *Bismarck* on 14 February 1939. Happy Valentine's Day, everyone. *Bismarck* was a mean machine. Sixty thousand tonnes of pure naval power, a symbol of German strength, and by the late spring of 1941 she set out on her first mission.

When the war arrived, *Hood* had been in service for 20 years. When she had first been built, she had been state-of-the-art. During the interwar period, she had even been sent on a round-the-world tour, ostensibly to thank the Commonwealth nations for their help during the First World War, but also to remind the world that Britain still ruled the waves. She was world famous, a symbol of Britain's maritime might, but had spent so much time showing the flag that she hadn't been maintained, updated and repaired as well as she should. By the time of the Second World War she was out of date, and although still a fine ship wasn't a match for vessels such as the *Bismarck*. In May 1941 the *Bismarck* was engaged by the *Hood* in the Denmark Strait between Greenland and Iceland. The *Hood* was sunk. Only three members of the crew survived; Arthur and Bertie were not among them. (The incident famously caused Churchill to order, 'Sink the *Bismarck*.' A few days later she was crippled by aircraft launched from HMS *Ark Royal*, and then sunk by Royal Navy ships.)

As I prepared to embark on HMS *Northumberland*, I

couldn't help thinking about Pop, and about Arthur and Bertie. Would they have been surprised that seven decades after their deaths the transport of goods by sea continued to be of such importance? Probably not. Would they have been surprised that the British navy was once again hunting pirates? Perhaps. And what would they have made of the new breed of warship, with all its sophisticated and advanced weaponry, that was being tasked to patrol these waters?

Ever since the risk of piracy in the Gulf of Aden started to increase, there has been a concerted international effort to curb the number of incidents. This effort has taken the form of several operations, including Combined Task Force 151 and Operation Atalanta. It was as part of Operation Atalanta that HMS *Northumberland* was patrolling these waters. It was the first time that a Royal Navy warship had been tasked to fight pirates since 1816, when the British finally quelled the threat of the Barbary corsairs.

When the Somali pirates started hitting the headlines, the trouble was this. International military vessels patrolling the Indian Ocean would hear news of an attack and make chase. The pirates, though, were cute to the intricacies of international diplomacy. They would speed back into Somali waters knowing that, without permission from the interim Somali government, foreign naval vessels were unwilling to follow. The pirates would be home and dry before they were either home or dry. If the international community was to be of any help at all, the Somali government needed to make an official request, and allow military vessels from other nations to enter its waters. That request finally came in June 2008.

Operation Atalanta is a joint naval patrol comprising around 20 ships from several member nations of the European Union, although it has its headquarters in Northwood, England. It operates alongside Combined Task Forces 151 – an American-led patrol – and 150. CTF-150 had in fact been patrolling these waters for some years in an anti-terrorist action. Large quantities of weapons are illegally transported through the Gulf of Aden; moreover, Somalia and Yemen are suspected hideouts for al-Qaeda, and Pirate Alley is their escape route. So that was another thing to worry about. Between them, Operation Atalanta and CTF-150 and -151 had put a lot of naval might in the Gulf of Aden, but there's a hell of a lot of water to patrol, and the pirates still slip through the net.

HMS *Northumberland* is a Type 23 frigate. There are 13 Type 23s in the Royal Navy, each of them named after British dukes, which is why they're also known as Duke-class vessels. Originally designed as anti-submarine warships, they are now the mainstay of the navy's surface fleet and can operate anywhere in the world. Type 23 frigates have two Rolls-Royce engines not unlike those that once powered Concorde, which are used to get the ship from A to B very quickly. They burn a lot of fuel, however, and are very noisy. If you're hunting submarines, that noise is going to give you away, so in addition they have four quieter engines mounted on rubber to absorb the throb. So these warships might look big and cumbersome, but in fact they're incredibly quiet and manoeuvrable when they need to be.

It costs well over £10 million a year to keep *Northumberland* shipshape, but you get a lot of bang for your buck. The frigate is loaded with a formidable arsenal: two quad

Harpoon surface-to-surface missile launchers, a vertical-launch Sea Wolf anti-missile system, a 4.5-inch Mark 8 naval gun, two 30-millimetre close-range guns, two anti-submarine torpedo tubes, a NATO Seagnat (a decoy system used to protect against incoming missiles) and DLF3 decoy launchers. It sounds like a lot – it *is* a lot – but the ship needs it: if she comes under attack from an enemy surface-to-surface missile, which whizzes across the water like a skimming stone, she has the grand total of four seconds to react to the incoming fire.

Northumberland also carries a Merlin Mark 1 helicopter. This helicopter is also primarily for anti-submarine operations, but its state-of-the-art sonics and sonar systems mean it's ideally suited for anti-surface ops. The Merlin is designed to be used in adverse weather and 'high-sea states'. It has a maximum speed of 167 knots (that's about 190 miles per hour) and is armed with Sting Ray torpedoes or depth charges – a kind of underwater bomb. ('Depth charges' is also naval slang for a bowl of stewed figs – gives you an idea of the sort of effect the weapons have . . .) A general purpose machine gun (GPMG) can be mounted in five different locations throughout the cabin so that it can be aimed through the doors or windows. Merlin has enough fuel to operate within a radius of 200 nautical miles. All in all, a serious piece of kit. As well as its current maritime duties, it's seen plenty of active service – both in Iraq and in the Caribbean on anti-narcotics and hurricane-support ops.

I didn't quite know what to expect when I met up with the frigate where it was docked in the port of Salalah on the coast of Oman – 100 miles from the coast of Yemen and at the eastern end of the Gulf of Aden. I'd spent plenty of time with the British army, but the navy was a new one on me. One of the first things I noticed was that the area of the port around the ship was blocked off by huge metal containers piled up on each other. This was to stop potential suicide bombers approaching the vessel. Oman might have been a low-risk location, but it brought home to me that our notions of safety are all relative: even here nobody associated with a Royal Navy frigate could fully relax.

I was welcomed on board by the captain of the *Northumberland*, Lieutenant Commander Martin Simpson – a charming man with a clipped, British way of speaking. I was soaking wet as we met on the deck – not from seawater, but from sweat. Salalah is only a few degrees south of the equator, and the heat was almost crippling.

It was explained to me how the naval hierarchy of command works. The second in command is the executive officer, or XO. He runs the ship. The captain makes all the decisions about what the ship is going to do and where it's going to go. Martin was answerable to a Greek commander as Operation Atalanta involved an international fleet. The crew were nearing the end of a six-month deployment in the area. He told me that his greatest sense of achievement came not from hunting pirates, but from escorting food aid from the World Food Programme into Mogadishu – even though *Northumberland* could not actually enter the port itself for fear of being rocketed from the mainland.

Introductions made, the camera crew and I started looking around this impressive ship. What we found was something like a floating city. *Northumberland* produces its own electricity; it can desalinate a certain amount of its own water; and, of course, it must accommodate its crew for large stretches of time. At no point, however, could you ever forget that you're on a battleship. Below decks is like something from *Blade Runner*. No windows, just a maze of tiny metal corridors with flashing lights, ladders and buttons, a constant electrical hum in the air and the distant churning of the ship's engines. There are wooden blocks all over the place. These are there in the event of water flooding into the boat and entrances needing to be blocked off. They are more effective than metal barriers because wood bends under force rather than buckles. You need to be incredibly careful and skilled at going up and down the ladders and moving around the ship – I was forever tripping up and bashing myself around, and to this day parts of me still ache from my clumsiness. Poor me. It took me four days to work out the route from our cabin up to the bridge. Those grey, metallic corridors all look the same. Some of the ladders lead somewhere, others lead nowhere – or at least nowhere I wanted to go. Or was allowed to go. I felt like the new boy at school, always getting lost on his way to class.

I was barracked with five others in a warrant officers' dorm – cramped and tiny by anyone's standards, though hardly surprising given that the ship has a crew of about 200 men and women. At least in the army when you settle down for the night you've got room to dump your Bergen and spread out a bit. Not here. One bunk, one drawer and one little cupboard is all you have each. All your belongings have to be immaculately squared away and tied down so that they take up the minimum of space and don't go walkabout should the ship hit a rough patch. Our cabin couldn't have been more than six metres by six, and we were lucky:

in a warrant officers' dorm the bunks are only two high. Lower-ranking sailors have to put up with three or four bunks on top of each other. It makes a tin of sardines look positively roomy.

You might be surrounded by all the water you can see, but on a ship you have to be very careful about how much you use. It's not rationed, but everyone understands that the last thing a ship wants to do is run out, especially in the burning heat just south of the equator. At the end of the corridor was the toilet, or 'head', so called because sailors would traditionally do their business at the head of the ship, where the splashing water would naturally clean away their deposits (give me a bottle of Domestos any day). Now, though, it was below deck with us, its walls curved because it's pressed up against the hull of the ship, and hot because that's what modern ships are like.

When I arrived at my bunk I found a copy of *Private* magazine under the covers. For those of you unfamiliar with this highbrow publication, it's an intimate magazine for gentlemen, put there just in case the long lonely nights should prove too much for my libido. Thanks, lads. Much appreciated. Whether the lads themselves rely on such magazines, I couldn't say. I do know, however, that although relationships certainly occur on board ship, there's a strict no-shagging policy, and anyone caught in flagrante can expect a severe reprimand. I suppose you have to make sure that the boys and girls have their minds on the job in hand.

My hosts had also stuck a picture of my former on-screen better half Sharon and Roly the dog onto the underside of the bunk above – 'so you don't get homesick'. By now, though, I was well used to the military sense of humour and while there was the same piss-taking I'd had to undergo whenever I got to know a new bunch of soldiers in Afghanistan, most of the guys and girls on *Northumberland* had seen those documentaries and had liked them. It helped to break the ice – the guys and girls on board had a great deal of respect for what the army were going through, even if there was a vague sense of rivalry between them. Unlike in Afghanistan, alcohol was allowed on the ship. There's a limit of two cans of beer a day for regular sailors on their downtime, although they managed somehow to find enough supplies on one occasion to get *me* a little merrier than perhaps I should have been. After all, there's nothing funnier than a bloke off the telly getting hammered . . .

On a massive ship like this the biggest threat is not sinking – it is, after all, very hard to down a Type 23 frigate – but fire. If a fire somehow started on board, it could be disastrous, especially if it reached the network of corridors below deck. Fire needs oxygen to burn, so it will seek it out, causing deadly fireballs down those corridors. If you happen to be between the fireball and the oxygen it needs, you fry; and you can imagine the chaos and devastation a fire could cause when so many people are crammed into such a small place with no means of escape. Trouble is, a warship is packed to the rafters with things that *cause* fire: fuel, electrics, enough weaponry to take out a substantial chunk of north London. It means that fire regulations are of paramount importance. Everyone's aware of these regulations, and they follow them to the letter. Smoking, obviously, is a no-no below deck, and every time you go above you have to seal the hatch in order to limit the possible entrance points a fire can take. Many members of the crew wore white fire-retardant suits over their uniforms.

Even in the absence of fire, temperatures could be horribly high. *Northumberland*'s cooling system was a network of pipes carrying cold water. Just before we joined the ship, this cooling system had broken down – not good in such a hot environment, and it meant that everyone was cooking in their cabins. The ship never sleeps. Everyone on board is on a continuous rotation and there is a constant hubbub of activity as the crew goes about their business of keeping this floating town operational and, at the same time, performing their crucial military task: hunting for pirates.

There was a palpable sense of tension as *Northumberland* prepared to leave the relative security of Salalah. Some of that tension derived from the fact that manoeuvring a frigate out of port is a complicated business. Get it wrong and you can do some serious damage to a very expensive ship. All hands were on deck, and anxious sailors looked nervously over the side to check that everything was going as it should. After all, scraping a Type 23 isn't like scratching your mum's car. But the tension wasn't just down to the difficulty of moving this massive but strangely delicate ship out of harbour. Everyone was well aware that as soon as we moved out of Omani waters, we'd be in Pirate Alley. It didn't matter that we were aboard a Royal Navy warship. We'd be searching for dangerous men carrying dangerous weapons and you could sense the ship was moving from a relaxed state to an operational one.

As soon as we were out of harbour, I joined Commander Simpson up on the bridge. This is the hub of the ship, and it was alive with activity. Orders were given and carried out;

information came in over the radio to be processed and disseminated; bearings were taken; and a lookout kept constant watch over the surrounding water through a set of powerful binoculars. It was a hard-working, utilitarian place, but not without its comforts. Martin Simpson had engaged a friend of his who worked at an Aston Martin garage to make a seat for him – not exactly standard navy issue, but more comfortable (and more slick) for the boss's behind than whatever arrangement it replaced. The Aston Martin accessory took centre stage in the middle of the bridge. Simpson was chuffed to bits with it.

As we stood together on the bridge, he explained to me what his operational priorities were. Number one: to protect World Food Programme ships delivering food aid into Somalia. Number two: to protect other vulnerable shipping in the Gulf of Aden. Number three: to arrest pirates.

'Is there any particular environment,' I asked him, 'that the pirates prefer to operate in?'

The captain stretched out his hands and indicated the wide open ocean that we could see through the bridge window. The water was flat. Calm. Like a millpond. A vast merchant ship chugged in the distance.

'*This* environment,' he said. 'It's easier for them to board ships when the sea state is calm. The choppier the water is, the better it is for the merchant vessels.' Made sense.

I wanted to know what ships were most at risk. 'The vessels that have been pirated have all been slow and have a low freeboard – the distance from the water to a deck they can put a ladder on.'

I learned that a ship is unlikely to be pirated if it's travelling above 14 knots. Pirates are like burglars – they will go for the house where the latch isn't secure. Like burglars, they know that there are easy pickings out there, so why make life difficult for themselves? 'All the pirates will do,' the captain told me, 'is wait until they find something that *looks* promising.' As we stared out of the window I pointed out a vessel. Its freeboard seemed pretty high to me – certainly I didn't much fancy the idea of using a ladder placed precariously on a little boat many metres below to try and board it. 'Too high?' I asked the captain.

He shook his head. 'Low enough.' Pointing to another vessel, he explained that the freeboard on that would present more difficulties – to me it looked unnaturally high. I was beginning to get the impression that there was a lot of at-risk shipping out there – I'd only been on board a few minutes and I'd already seen some. HMS *Northumberland* and the rest of the Operation Atalanta fleet had their work cut out.

Having patrolled these waters for the past six months, Lieutenant Commander Simpson obviously knew a great deal about how modern pirates operate. I asked him what usually happened once they took control of a ship. 'The pirates themselves don't hurt in any way the crew of the vessels they've pirated,' he told me. 'We want that to continue. If we start taking down vessels that have been pirated, there is a very great risk that the innocent civilians will either be caught in crossfire or, at worst, executed.'

The captain of the *Northumberland*, then, and indeed those in charge of the rest of Operation Atalanta, had a difficult balance to strike between the threat of force and actually carrying it out. It struck me that all the advanced weaponry the ship was carrying could very well be redundant when it was faced with delicate hostage situations, that in the hunt for pirates, brain could be more important than brawn. That didn't mean, though, that the weapons systems weren't at the ready. While we were in Omani waters, the guns weren't allowed to be loaded, but the moment we crossed over onto open sea and into our patrol area, that changed. Ammo was inserted; weapons systems were activated. It wasn't long before the air above me turned to thunder and all around us the water exploded as rounds slammed into the sea – the ship's guns had to be test-fired to make sure they were fully operational. It was only a short demonstration of *Northumberland*'s firepower, but it was enough to make it clear that the frigate's arsenal was as impressive as I thought it would be.

Now that we had entered dangerous waters, the ship's crew were instructed to prepare for action stations – a state of readiness that means every single member of the crew, from the cooks to the captain, is ready to enter a battle situation. Every man and woman on the *Northumberland* needed to be able to switch to action stations at a moment's notice. Should that happen, off-duty members of the crew would have to report to their posts and the weapons systems would be placed on 'hot standby', which meant they would be ready to fire. Officers would make regular checks to ensure everyone was at their posts and ready to do battle. At action stations, though, the day-to-day running of this ship still had to go smoothly – meals, for example, would still have to be produced and so *Northumberland*'s cooks would be tested regularly on their ability to do this.

Action stations is exhausting for the crew. Keep it up for too long and they'll be knackered before you know it. And so they would maintain a state of advanced readiness, just below action stations, for as long as the frigate was patrolling Pirate Alley.

The majority of the crew of HMS *Northumberland* were not armed. There was, however, a small contingent of men carrying firearms. They were highly trained, and performed constant firearms exercises. These were, of course, Royal Marines. It was the Marines who would be on the front line of the battle against the pirates. With any luck, we'd be joining them in this battle, and having spent some time with their colleagues in Afghanistan, I wanted to get to know them as soon as possible.

The Marines on the frigate were part of the Fleet Protection Group Royal Marines (FPGRM). This elite commando force is a cadre of just over 500 soldiers whose responsibility is the security of Royal Navy assets, both at home and worldwide. Once known as the Comacchio Group, they were originally responsible for the protection of Britain's nuclear weapons and for counter-terrorist operations at sea. This latter role is now the responsibility of the SBS – the Special Boat Service – but the SBS continues to be backed up by the Fleet Protection Group. The FPGRM is divided into four squadrons: HQ headquarters squadron, O rifle squadron, R rifle squadron and S rifle squadron. Each of these is divided into several units, and the lads on board *Northumberland* were from the Fleet Standby Rifle Troop (FSRT), a high-readiness unit tasked to support the Royal Navy worldwide. FSRT teams have specialist weapons skills, and are specifically trained in 'non-compliant boarding skills'. (To you and me, that means getting on a boat when the pirates don't want you to – a dangerous occupation in this part of the world, but a crucial one.) The Fleet Protection Group can find themselves almost anywhere in the world – from the Arctic Circle to the equator.

The Marines I met were as fit as a butcher's dog. These guys spent a *lot* of time on the ship working out and were, they told me, a little frustrated not to have had the chance to fire their guns in a combat situation. To a man, they wished they had been posted to Afghanistan like some of their mates. I told them they were better off where they were, but it was a testament, I think, to their professionalism that they were eager to face up to whatever anyone could throw at them. The Marines constantly had to practise close-quarter battle techniques on board the ship. Sergeant Macaffer explained to me that it was impossible to drill these techniques too often: they had to be second nature to the team because they never knew when or under what circumstances they would have to use them.

The ship's captain had explained to me the difficulties involved in engaging a vessel that had been pirated. In addition, I knew from my time in Afghanistan that the military's actions are governed by their rules of engagement – the predetermined regulations that state when, where and how they are permitted to engage an enemy. In Helmand Province it was well known that Taliban fighters would put down their RPG launchers, pick up a hoe and pretend to be innocent villagers, and when that happened, the British army couldn't touch them – even if, minutes ago, they'd been trying to take the soldiers' lives. Commander Simpson had hinted at similar problems at sea, and I wanted to know exactly what the Marines' rules of engagement were. Once pirates were on a vessel and controlled the hostages, were the Marines allowed to exercise their 'non-compliant boarding skills'?

Sergeant Macaffer shook his head. 'No. If it's effectively a hostage situation where they've adopted a defensive posture and are threatening to take the lives of the crew, that's out of our jurisdiction.'

I could well imagine that it must be frustrating for these highly trained soldiers not to be able to use their well-honed expertise to deal with dangerous hostage situations. At the same time I could see the problems involved. The pirates in the Gulf of Aden tended not to kill their captives, and as Sergeant Macaffer succinctly put it, 'We don't want to force the issue.'

It was becoming clear to me that there was only a small window of time during which the forces of HMS *Northumberland* – and therefore I – would be able to catch up with any pirates, and that was when they were actually in the process of boarding a target vessel. In order to capture them at that crucial moment, we needed to be in that part of the Gulf of Aden where they were likely to be most highly concentrated. Where the action was, and the danger.

And so it was that we set sail for the corridor.

4. The Corridor

Shipping convoys have been around for a very long time, and for very good reasons. Safety in numbers is one; ease of military protection is another. During the Second World War, the British made it compulsory for all merchant ships to travel in convoy along specific routes so the Royal Navy could more readily offer them protection against German surface ships and U-boats. The Germans soon developed anti-convoy tactics, but convoys were still better than the alternative – ships dotted willy-nilly around the ocean, easy targets for enemy strikes. When the Americans joined the war and refused to use convoys along their eastern seaboard, the German U-boats had a field day. The Americans were finally forced to follow the British example, and convoys became the norm for the remainder of the conflict.

Maritime technology might have come a long way in the intervening 60 years, but a lot of things have stayed the same, and the convoy system is one of them. Any merchant shipping travelling through the Gulf of Aden is advised to follow a particular route. They queue up at the end of this narrow corridor, then travel together through it. This stops the merchant vessels from being spread out all over a million square miles of sea and allows naval ships and air support to patrol a more concentrated area of ocean.

There is just one problem. The existence of the corridor

not only tells the warships of Operation Atalanta where the merchant vessels are congregating, it tells the pirates too, and some of them flock to the corridor like wasps to jam. It seemed to me that the corridor didn't reduce the number of Somali pirates in the Gulf of Aden, it just forced them to operate in a smaller area. And it was to that area that we were headed. (Other pirates have worked out that ships queuing up at the end of the corridor to travel through the Gulf of Aden together have to have come from somewhere and that it's impossible to police all the world's oceans. And so they simply move their area of operations. If you look at maps on which piracy hot spots have been charted from year to year, you'll see that they change location. It's like cutting the heads off the hydra – remove one and another grows somewhere else.)

As the sun set on our first day on board HMS *Northumberland*, a radio operator sent out a message to all shipping in the Gulf: 'All stations. All stations. All stations. This is coalition warship Foxtrot 23. We are conducting maritime security operations within the Gulf of Aden. Anyone witnessing any criminal or suspicious activities are to contact coalition warship on channel 16.'

Channel 16. The international distress channel. Monitored day and night by coastguards around the world and used only for broadcasting distress calls. The radio operators on *Northumberland* would be keeping constant, careful tabs on channel 16 for as long as we were in Pirate Alley, waiting for the call that meant a merchant ship was being boarded by pirates. Whether that call came or not was anyone's guess. We just had to wait and see.

*

Darkness. My first night on board. The stars above were blindingly bright, a breathtaking canopy out here in the middle of the ocean where there was no ambient light to make them dim. But out to sea it was impenetrably black. Anything could be going on out there.

The sun might have gone down, but it was still hot on deck thanks to the winds blowing off the deserts of Africa and the Arabian Gulf. I was sweating even as I peered into the gloom, wondering what was out there waiting for us. I knew that most pirate attacks took place at dawn or dusk, but I also knew that when you're dealing with dangerous, unpredictable people like this, the one thing you have to expect is the unexpected. The crew of *Northumberland*, on constant rotation, would not be letting their guard slip for a minute. And aboard the merchant ships in the Gulf of Aden the cover of darkness wouldn't bring much comfort . . .

And then word reached me that we were just about to enter the corridor. I made my way to the bridge to speak to one of the guys. He showed me a navigation screen, glowing blue in the darkness and with our position and that of the corridor clearly marked. It was 50 nautical miles to the south-west. 'As you go past Aden,' he told me, 'you get a lot of vessels that look like pirate vessels, so we'll stick to the north of the corridor because the merchant traffic does tend to get a bit nervous around there.' I bet they do.

It would take us around 40 hours to travel the length of the corridor. Two days, two nights, as near as damn it. I tried to imagine what it must be like for a merchant ship travelling that route, knowing that they could be boarded by pirates with RPGs at any moment. Not for the first time, I felt a sense of relief that I was on board a Royal Navy frigate and not one of those vulnerable vessels.

With that thought going through my head, I turned in for the night, genuinely not knowing what the next few days would bring.

In Afghanistan I had learned that war was characterized by long stretches of boredom, punctuated by moments of sudden activity (and in the Stan, blind fear). The fight against the pirates wasn't much different – acts of terror on the high seas don't tend to happen where and when you want them. In a million square miles of ocean it's difficult to be in the right place at the right time and there's a lot of nervous waiting around. So it was not until my third day on board HMS *Northumberland* that the call came in. Captain Andy Morris of the Fleet Protection Group Royal Marines was called to the bridge for a briefing and I went with him. There was a large group of Somali boats, or dhows, in the vicinity, surrounded by a significant number of skiffs – long flat boats of the type favoured both by Somali fishermen and by Somali pirates. 'My intention,' Simpson told the Marine unit leader, 'is to perform an approach-and-assist visit on that group.'

Andy Morris nodded. He had his orders, and left the bridge to brief his men.

The Fleet Protection Group congregated on deck. They wore desert camouflage gear and life jackets, along with Osprey body armour and Gecko Marine Safety Helmets. A couple of the guys carried the short version of the SA80 assault rifle. The standard version would be too long because in the event of them having to board a large ship, they would have to go round tight corners. (I learned that the shortened SA80 is also used by tank crews so that they can get in and out of their vehicles more easily.) Other members of the FPG carried Heckler & Koch MP5 submachine guns – predominantly a special forces weapon and more suited to the job in hand. The 556 round from an SA80 has more velocity behind it than the 9-millimetre from the MP5. This can be hazardous in a close-quarter battle situation: the 556 can go through a body and still bounce around the room like a rubber ball in a tin can. The rigid inflatable boats (RIBs) themselves were mounted with general purpose machine guns. All in all, everyone was pretty heavily armed.

Andy explained to me that it was commonplace in these waters for tuna fishermen to tow skiffs behind the slightly bigger dhows, and these skiffs usually had about 12 people on board. Unfortunately, this was exactly what the pirates do as well. Often the dhows will have been pirated in the first place, and the fishermen thrown overboard. The pirates will then stay out to sea for up to 40 days, watching and waiting for a suitable target to cross their path. I guess when you have the prospect of such a big payday coming your way, you don't mind hanging around for a while . . .

From a distance, the dhows we were about to approach looked just like innocent fishing boats. Fly over the Gulf of Aden and you'll see plenty of these boats, many of them sailed by legitimate Somali fishermen earning their living from the tuna-rich waters of the area. There were ways, however, of distinguishing fishermen from pirates. 'They've got equipment that they use for getting on board other vessels, and that's the key,' Andy told me. 'It's the ladders – you can't hide a ladder on a skiff.' And obviously, if you have a ladder out at sea, it's not so that you can go and clean windows. 'If we see grappling hooks,' Andy continued, 'and obviously weapons . . .'

'Fishermen don't have rocket-propelled grenades,' I suggested.

Andy grinned. 'Exactly,' he said. 'It's a bit of a giveaway.'

The Marines would approach the skiffs in their RIBs. Two members of the group would be ready to act as snipers from the Merlin helicopter, which could be called into action should things kick off. One of these snipers would be armed with an AW50 rifle. This is a serious bit of weaponry, as I had found out in Afghanistan when, more than once, its rounds flew just over my head. The sniper wouldn't use his 50-cal to take out people; instead it would be used, should the situation require it, against engine blocks, a technique that's used a lot in anti-narcotics operations out in the West Indies. Hit a small boat's engine with one of those rounds, which can have either explosive or armour-piercing tips, and there really won't be a lot left of it.

As the Marines, accompanied by some regular navy guys, prepared to disembark from *Northumberland* and speed in their RIBs towards the suspicious vessels, you could tell that this was a well-practised routine for them. There was just one small difference this time round: they'd have a couple of extra passengers, namely me and Will, the cameraman. It wasn't just the Marines that had to get their gear together. We did too. I'd been told before I left England that if I had body armour, I should bring it along, so I had it wrapped around my torso and a helmet firmly on my head. I was also carrying camera batteries and tapes so that Will had a bit less to deal with. You don't get a very stable ride travelling at 25 knots on a RIB (understatement of the decade), and it's kind of difficult to get a steady shot. I was also wearing a life jacket. I'd had it explained to me that some life jackets inflate on contact with water, which sounds like a good idea, especially if you're knocked unconscious into the water. But they have their downsides. If you're underwater and your life jacket inflates automatically, you rise to the top no matter what's above you (and in a military environment the thing above you can be sharp and dangerous). In situations like that, it's much safer, if you can manage it, to swim out of the way of any hazards on the surface and then inflate your life jacket manually. So it was that we had been equipped with toggle-inflating jackets.

I watched as a group of Marines embarked and then sped off in their RIB, and then it was my turn. To get onto the RIB from the deck of *Northumberland* involves climbing down a rope ladder. It looks easy, but it's not: as the hull of the ship curves inwards towards the bottom, you're not only going down, you're also at a precarious angle. Nothing too dramatic, but enough to make it tricky if, like me, you're unused to the process – and enough to make you look like a prize prick if you lose your footing and end up in the drink. More to the point, there are plenty of sharp, jagged bits of kit in the RIB below that you really don't want to fall on top of. (During our stay on *Northumberland*, one of our party came a cropper doing this and got such severe rope burn that it cut right through the skin of his hand.) As I struggled down the ladder from the moving deck of the *Northumberland* onto the wobbling RIB, I felt I was having a brief taster of how difficult it must be for pirates to board the ships they target.

Once the RIB was loaded, I grabbed hold of something to keep my balance in the gently billowing water, and then we were off.

We headed towards the suspect vessels at speed and the plan was this. We would approach the first dhow and one of the boats would hold off at a slight distance and offer fire support from the GPMG. The other guys would approach the sailors and ask if they could board their vessel. Nothing like the direct approach. The white foam on either side of the speeding RIB splashed and sprayed as the sun beat down from the clear blue sky. Under other circumstances, it could almost have been idyllic. Almost, but not quite – most people don't take GPMGs and MP5s on holiday with them.

The RIBs started to slow down, the spray decreased and I caught my first sight of the potential pirates. There were nine or ten of them, sitting quietly on a skiff and staring at us with unknowable, almost blank expressions on their faces. Their skin was dark and they wore an odd assortment of clothes: some had traditional headdresses and ethnic garb; others wore old sweatshirts with Western logos. A lot of them were very young, but their skiff was rickety and old. Parts of it were brightly painted, but in general it had a functional, utilitarian feel. The occupants looked poor. They looked wary. What they didn't look like was pirates. Even I could tell that without any knowledge of what pirates looked like.

Andy tried to speak to them, using basic Arabic, but they

didn't respond. One of the guys opened up a little box and held up a small plastic bag filled with a handful of tiny fish. 'We're fisherman,' he appeared to be trying to say. Well, perhaps, but it was a minuscule catch for a lot of guys. It seemed obvious to me, and to everyone else, that the fish we were being shown were food, even though the Somalis in general are not big fish-eaters. (They prefer a slice of camel meat, washed down with camel milk. I think I'll stick to cod and chips myself.) But whatever these people's foodie preferences were, we started to suspect that the boat we had encountered was run not by fishermen, nor even pirates, but by purveyors of another kind of illegality that plagues the Gulf of Aden, another community of seafarers. You'd be hard pressed to find a more desperate, treacherous bunch anywhere in the world.

I'd already learned that Somalia was a war-torn, dangerous place. What I didn't know was the lengths to which the Somali poor would go in order to get the hell out of there. Where there's a will, there's a way; and where there's a need, there's money to be made. The plight of these citizens has given rise to a booming trade in people smuggling, and the human tragedy involved in this sorry business is almost immeasurable.

Hundreds of people a week make the dangerous voyage across the Gulf of Aden to Yemen. They are not always Somalis, but also come from Ethiopia, Sudan or even further afield. Driven from their homes by drought, economic hardship, the threat of violence or – most probably – all three, these men, women and children are willing to risk everything in search of a better life in Yemen and the Middle East. Yemen, though, is hardly a refugee's paradise. On the contrary. It's one of the five remaining countries in the world where the execution of juvenile offenders is still permitted; arbitrary arrests – especially in the south – are commonplace and there is widespread judicial corruption. Freedom of speech, freedom of the press and freedom of religion are all highly restricted. In short, Yemen is a brutal, difficult place to live. But it's still better than Somalia.

A substantial proportion of the refugees, however, don't even make it as far as the Yemeni coast. The people smugglers charge a fee of around £20 per person – doesn't sound like a lot, but it's an almost impossible sum for a Somali refugee – and pack them tightly into their tiny boats. The smugglers, however, are not exactly full of the milk of human kindness. They frequently overload their boats – the more money they can earn from a crossing, the better – before setting sail. If, as often happens, they get out into the open water and the boat is too heavy on account of their greed, these enterprising businessmen simply dump part of their load. There have been reports of pregnant women and children being unceremoniously chucked into the water, and of course they have no hope of surviving.

Yemen has more than 80,000 Somali refugees. It mounts constant coastguard patrols throughout its waters in an attempt to locate the smugglers. This only has a limited effect. If the smugglers see the coastguard – or a vessel that they think *might* be a coastguard – they do what any professional criminal would do: get rid of the evidence. If that means throwing a whole boatload of refugees overboard, so be it.

You'd think that the dangers involved, along with the smugglers' sense of customer service, would dissuade refugees from paying their £20 and risking everything to get to Yemen. Not a bit of it. They're queuing up to get out of Somalia. They risk it in their thousands. I'm told that if you walk along the northern coast of Somalia, it won't be long until you come across a shoe. Or a belt. Or a jacket. The non-human remains of humans long gone, drowned somewhere between the Somali and Yemeni coasts, their bodies rotted away or eaten by fish.

Were these Yemeni people smugglers that we had encountered? It was impossible to say for sure but it certainly seemed likely. From the RIB, Andy continued trying to talk to them. Without an interpreter it was difficult – none of them spoke English and his Arabic was basic – but gradually he managed to tease out some information. He pointed at a small hatch that led into the hull of the boat and indicated that he wanted a member of the skiff's crew to open it up. One of them did so, removing a piece of rush matting before he could raise the hatch.

There were people sleeping underneath. 'How many?' Andy asked.

A shuffling kind of pause. One of the passengers held up five fingers, but without boarding the skiff you couldn't say if he was telling the truth or not.

Andy radioed through to *Northumberland* and reported what we had found. 'Sixteen people on board, one child that we can see. They've got a fair amount of fuel on board and they say they're from Yemen.'

Back on the bridge of the *Northumberland*, Lieutenant Commander Martin Simpson listened carefully, all the while speaking into a Dictaphone so that he had a legal record of the encounter. Everything had to be done very strictly by the book. 'Do not board,' he instructed, 'until I give a direct order.'

'Roger,' Andy replied, and slowly the RIBs started to withdraw from the vicinity of the Yemeni boats.

As the RIBs filled with Marines and guns bobbed around the boats, Andy gave me the low-down. 'That's a lot of people,' he told me, 'for that size dhow with one skiff.'

So could they be running people?

He nodded curtly. 'Yeah,' he stated. 'That's exactly what they could be doing. This is prime space, in between Somalia and Yemen. What I'd like to do is get on board and see if they've got any ID. We've had reports in the past they've seen the coastguard coming out, they obviously don't want to be caught with people so they're fairly ruthless and just chuck them overboard.'

The Marines might have had the upper hand in terms of the force they could exert, but even with their firepower the intricacies of international diplomacy on the high seas meant they couldn't just board this tiny 'fishing' vessel at will. Royal Marines boarding a ship from another nation could cause a stink and they had to follow certain protocols. Andy and the Fleet Protection Group first needed permission from the commander of *Northumberland*; he, in turn, needed to get the go-ahead from HQ back in the UK.

While we waited for permission to board, we approached another skiff which had so much old clothing draped over its beams that it looked like a floating laundry. 'Fishermen are normally pretty proud of their catch,' Andy explained as we drifted towards them. 'Normally when we come along-

side them, they'll get the fish out and show us straightaway.'
But we were getting no impromptu fish counters to look at;
just a wary greeting from the many desperate-looking individuals on this second boat.

'*Salam*,' they called.

'*Salam*,' we replied, in our pidgin Arabic.

They waved at us as we drew alongside them. Andy
asked what they were doing. In response, one of them
handed over a beaten-up old block of polystyrene with a
length of knotted twine wrapped around it and, at the
end, the rustiest hook I'd ever seen in my life. These
people *could* have been fishermen, but you'd have more
luck tickling trout than trying your luck with that kind of
tackle. They weren't fooling anyone, not that it seemed
to bother them. Perhaps they were emboldened by the
fact that we hadn't boarded the previous skiff. I don't
know. What I *do* know is that at one end of the skiff was
a group of ten or eleven young men – children, really –
looking exhausted in the brutal heat of the day. I later
found out that the younger Somali refugees are, the more
chance they have of finding work in Yemen. They are
stronger and have more stamina. They can be worked
into the ground for a slave's wage and are less likely to
get ill or die. It seemed probable that this was the fate
that awaited these youngsters when and if they finally
made it across Pirate Alley.

Permission to board the skiffs never arrived, so we were
unable to investigate any further. There was no sign that
they were transporting drugs or arms and we couldn't prove
that they were people smugglers. Even if we could, what
would we do with them? Where would we take them? Dump

them back on the coastline? That wouldn't be a great idea: if refugees find themselves in an area controlled by a rival clan they'll probably be killed; if not, they'll immediately be out on the water again, trying to get to Yemen. I had the impression that the crews of these boats knew that they would be dealt with softly by the British navy. Had we been the Yemeni or Omani coastguard, on the other hand, I suspect the smugglers' attitude would have been somewhat different – and possibly terminal for the refugees. I'd heard that in parts of Yemen convicted pirates could still be cruci-fied. I don't know what the punishment is for people smuggling, but I somehow doubt it's just a fine and an ASBO, and all the evidence suggests that Yemeni people smugglers will go to any lengths to avoid being caught by the wrong authorities.

That didn't include us, however. The Marines were RTB'd – returned to boat – and as we sped back to HMS *Northumberland* I had the distinct feeling that we had just witnessed one of the more unsavoury consequences of the chaos and hardship occurring in Somalia. Whatever the truth, everyone was pretty sure they weren't fishermen.

And I was also starting to realize something else, some-thing that was to become increasingly clear to me as my global search for pirates progressed. The Somali refugees I had just encountered, if indeed that is what they were, were only on the water because of what was happening in Somalia itself. If I was going to understand why piracy is so widespread, maybe I would have to look at what was happening not only out at sea, but also on land.

I didn't have much time to think about this, however, because just then a call came through. Some more suspicious boats had been reported to HMS *Northumberland*, but this time they were out of range of the RIBs. The Merlin helicopter was being prepped for flight, and if we wanted to find out what was going down, we needed to be on it.

5. Distress Call

The rotary blades of the Merlin were already spinning as I gingerly climbed out of the RIB, up the rope ladder and back onto the deck of *Northumberland*. It's only when you get up close to a helicopter on a flight deck that you realize how skilled these pilots must be. There's not a lot of room, even on a frigate of this size. Not much margin for error when you're coming in to land. I waited, a bit apprehensively, only metres away from this impressive piece of machinery while it was readied for take-off and then, when everything was prepped, Will the cameraman and I were given the thumbs up. We loaded ourselves in, and within seconds we were rising into the air.

The Gulf of Aden opened out before us, and HMS *Northumberland* disappeared from view. With the advantage of height I started to get some sense of the geographical problem facing the pirate hunters. Water as far as the eye could see and beyond the horizon, more water. Ships were dotted around below us, but even though there were many of them, they were insignificant compared to the vastness of ocean.

We sped through the skies. From up here, you can never rely on the naked eye to see what is happening on the water, but as the Merlin is primarily designed for anti-surface ship and anti-submarine warfare, tracking, surveillance and search-and-rescue missions, it's essential that the crew have good location and imaging capabilities. For this reason, the Merlin is equipped with both an over-the-horizon targeting radar and an extremely sensitive high-quality camera.

The radar is a bowl on the underside of the Merlin and is operated by a member of the crew. As soon as he picks up a vessel he assigns a track to it, and the camera operator can then target the vessel with his imaging machinery. This brings up clear images on the six high-definition colour displays in the cockpit of what is happening miles away. It needs to be powerful, of course, in order to pick up the periscope of a submarine's conning tower – little more than a dot in the ocean – and as we flew in the vicinity of a huge merchant ship, the camera operator, Tiny, showed me how he could pick out individual people on its deck using this high-tech equipment. He explained to me that this capability is particularly useful when you're going up against little fishing dhows of the type normally used by pirates, because you can get a good idea of who they are and what they're carrying, and on the basis of that information can decide whether to call for assistance from the ship, with a view to doing a boarding if necessary. Everything picked up by the camera was being recorded for the purpose of evidence.

We hadn't been in the air long when a dot came up on the radar screen. 'Left, 11 o'clock, four miles. We've got something in the water.'

'Roger. I've got a very faint radar contact but not a lot. If you can close it and try and get visuals on it . . .'

The camera zoomed in. This ship might have been some distance away, but the image on the screen was impressively clear. It was a dhow, churning through the water with four skiffs trailing behind it. And as I had already learned, that was a classic pirate set-up. From our position up in the skies the camera continued to focus on the dhow. The image was crystal. We saw a canopy flapping in the wind and a sturdy metal fishing rod leaning out over the water. No ladders. No grappling hooks. No weapons. The guys on the dhow, even to my untutored eye, were pretty obviously fishermen, just out there trying to make an honest living. They were allowed to go on their way without any further interference from us. It wasn't the first time that I'd been left to reflect that hunting pirates in the Gulf of Aden wasn't the easiest way to spend your time . . .

We continued our patrol, high above the corridor where 60 merchant vessels travel through the Gulf every day. I could see them clearly from this vantage point – huge industrial chunks of metal ploughing on like enormous workhorses. The crew pointed one out to me. 'They're obviously a bit twitched about pirates in the area,' Tiny told me. 'He's got his hoses out at the moment. That's to deter them.'

From the top of the freeboard, huge streams of water were pumping out of the ship into the surrounding sea. Tiny explained to me that generators are used to suck vast amounts of seawater in before spitting it out of the side as a deterrent. I could well understand that trying to come alongside a boat with those things thundering at you could put you off your shopping trip. At the same time, I'd come to the conclusion that the pirates in these waters were nothing if not ballsy. I wouldn't put it past them to give it a go even under these circumstances.

But not today. We continued our patrol for a while longer, then returned to *Northumberland*, our pilot putting us down perfectly on the flight deck. I couldn't help marvelling at his skill at touchdown even more than when we took off – the Merlin only just fits on the deck. At the same time I was a bit disappointed that our flight had come to nothing. It had been an eventful day, but by the end of it I was left frustrated that so far our search for pirates had been unsuccessful.

We woke early the following day, though to look at the activity on the ship you'd never have known the sun had only just risen: the corridors were bustling, just as I knew they would have been all night – the mini-city that is HMS *Northumberland* doesn't go to bed just because it's dark. So too were the decks. Groups of Royal Navy sailors kept their fitness up to scratch by jogging round the ship; the guys from the Fleet Protection Group dismantled and cleaned their weapons. They may not have had call to use them, but that didn't mean their SA80s and MP5s didn't have to be in perfect working order. Mechanics were at work before the heat of the day became too intense. A warship is constantly being fixed, tampered with, twiddled and twoddled (although I'm not sure if those are the precise technical terms). It's a sensitive piece of kit that requires constant expert maintenance.

I grabbed a quick breakfast before joining Commander Simpson on the bridge for an update on what had happened overnight. Nothing in terms of piracy, he told me. We looked at his chart which mapped the flow of shipping up and down the corridor. It was a busy old place but that didn't guarantee that we'd find ourselves any pirates. I continuously had to remind myself that robberies are unpredictable events, whether you're on land or sea. I was glad, of course, that nobody had been pirated over the past couple of days, but I couldn't keep the nagging disappointment at bay that so far our search had been unsuccessful. I asked the ship's commander, straight out, what the chances were of us coming into contact with pirates.

'There's every chance,' he told me firmly, before indicating the shipping map again. 'If you're a pirate, there's a lot of trade out there.'

He was right. What none of us knew at the time, however, was that things weren't going to pan out quite the way anyone expected.

To pass the time, I decided to go and chat with some of the junior ratings, the rank and file of *Northumberland*'s crew. I wanted to know what the ordinary sailors thought about the job that they were being tasked to do. We met in the 45-man mess, so called because, surprise surprise, 45 men live in it. They were a friendly, welcoming bunch, and I asked how many of them thought, when they joined the Royal Navy, that they'd be tasked with looking for pirates. They all shook their heads – all of them, that is, apart from one bright spark. 'I did, I must admit,' he announced. 'But then again I joined in 1640.' Give that man a prize!

I pointed out to the lads that it was costing a great deal of money to keep them out here in the Gulf of Aden. Was it worth it? Weren't our resources better used elsewhere. One of them shrugged. 'You're pretty much damned if you do and damned if you don't,' he said. 'If you *do* go and investigate skiffs and it just turns out to be fishermen, you could be seen as hassling them. But if you didn't go and investigate and it turned out to be a piracy attack, then they would look and say, what's the point of you actually being here?'

A pretty succinct distillation of the problem, I thought. But what of the pirates themselves? There are two sides to every story, and was it possible, while deploring their actions, to have sympathy for their motives? The people of Somalia are, after all, very, *very* poor. Mr 1640 gave his opinion.

'I see their point of view,' he said, 'because they've got families to feed. And they think the only way they can do it, because they've had no government for 20 years and all the rest of it, is to go out and rob some vessels. But I've got a family to feed. I don't go round pointing guns at people.'

A pause.

'Well,' he added, 'I do . . .'

Everyone laughed, me included. In a funny kind of way, however, this light-hearted comment had highlighted the problem well. Piracy is a serious criminal act, and like many criminal acts it is being dealt with by the threat of force. That doesn't mean to say, however, that some pirates aren't driven by genuine necessity. The World Bank estimates that about three-quarters of Somalis live on less than two US dollars a day. One of the few industries they have is fishing. The Gulf of Aden has traditionally been rich in tuna and other valuable fish. With worldwide fish stocks plummeting as a result of overfishing, the relative riches of the Gulf of Aden have attracted illegal trawlers. Foreign ships have made a beeline for the Gulf, hoovering up the precious fish stocks – to the tune of $300 million worth a year – to sell around the world, destroying the livelihood of these Somali fishermen before their very eyes.

The destruction of Somalia's fishing industry is not the only seaborne indignity the country has had to suffer at the hands of greedy foreign nations ready to take advantage of the political upheavals in the area. Another example has been going on for many years, but did not fully come home to roost until the Asian tsunami of 2004. Somalia is almost 3,000 miles away from the epicentre of the earthquake which caused that tsunami, but the effect on the country was devastating nevertheless. Accurate official figures do not exist, but it's thought that nearly 300 people were killed by the coastal damage and more than 50,000 were displaced. The region of Puntland took the lion's share of the damage, and that is the area of Somalia from which most of the pirates originate.

The tsunami was disastrous enough in itself, but it also uncovered a dirty little secret of the Somali coast. When the waters subsided, they left behind debris carried in from the sea. This debris included rusty steel drums, barrels and a range of other containers, many of them smashed open by the force of the tides. These containers held vast quantities of toxic waste – waste that foreign countries had been dumping off the coast of Somalia for more than a decade. Why Somalia? As usual, it comes down to the green stuff. To get rid of toxic waste in Europe is expensive – around the $250-a-ton mark. To dump it off the coast of Somalia costs $2.50. You do the math.

These containers of toxic waste are more than just an eyesore. They contain all manner of harmful materials – radioactive uranium, lead, heavy metals such as cadmium and mercury, hospital waste, chemical waste . . . The list goes on, and none of it's the sort of thing you want ending up on your beaches. The effect of this waste on health is terrible. Since the containers washed ashore there have been many reports of locals falling ill with symptoms that you might reasonably expect to be associated with such substances – bleeding from the mouth and abdomen, for example. There's no real way of proving that these symptoms stem from exposure to the toxic waste, if only because there's no one brave enough to set foot in Somalia to investigate it fully, but the correlation between the waste and the illnesses seems obvious enough to me.

Although it was the Asian tsunami that highlighted this problem, both to the Somalis and to the world, there had been rumours it was happening for a number of years. In 1994 an Italian journalist by the name of Ilaria Alpi travelled to Somalia to investigate. She claimed that the Italian Mafia was behind a large chunk of the toxic waste dumping, and it has been estimated that the Mafia is behind about 30 per cent of Italy's waste disposal. It was to be the last investigation the journalist ever made. She and her cameraman were killed in Somalia. Word on the street is that they were assassinated. By the Mafia? By Somali warlords? By any of the many people with a vested interest in keeping this business alive? Who knows, but it seems clear that a major international criminal organization was polluting the Somali coast without any thought for the people of that country. And it wasn't like they didn't have enough to deal with already.

Their livelihoods taken from them, their land poisoned, it would have been naive to expect the Somali fishermen to take this sitting down. They armed themselves, took to their boats and started patrolling the area. Some of them tried to scare foreign shipping away; others tried to levy a 'tax' on them. These fishermen did not see themselves as pirates, but as an unofficial coastguard, there to stop their waters being destroyed in the same way as their land had been. From these beginnings, the piracy epidemic spread. This is not to say that there are not gangsters, opportunists and out-and-out criminals among the pirates of Somalia. There are. Many of the pirates of Somalia are, relatively speaking, wealthy men, happy to use the wrongdoings of other nations as an excuse for their actions. But the truth about the origins of piracy in the area is not black and white. As usual, it is shades of grey.

1500 hours.

What looked like being a quiet day was suddenly hotting up. Two small unidentified vessels had been picked up on the radar. Nobody knew who they were or what they were doing, and so Lieutenant Commander Simpson had ordered the Fleet Protection Group and the Merlin to go and investigate. The already busy corridors of *Northumberland* became suddenly busier as we prepared ourselves for the off.

The Marines loaded themselves into their RIBs while I joined the Merlin crew and once more took off into the skies. The two Marine snipers in the helicopter took up position by their weapons – one with a GPMG, capable of firing a lot of rounds and designed to take out people, the other with an AW50 50-cal rifle designed to take out the engine block. Each weapon had a piece of black material attached to its side, the purpose of which was to stop the casings of discharged ammunition from pinging back into the Merlin. Those casings are very hot, and you want a fire on a helicopter even less than you want a fire on a boat . . .

Down on the water, the RIBs started circling one of the two skiffs. Everyone on the boats put their hands up. They were a ragtag bunch – men, women and children, all poorly dressed and with expressions of confused despair on their faces. It was clear from a single look that these were yet more refugees, unfortunate Africans risking the dangers of being smuggled across the water to Yemen.

The Merlin circled the second skiff, but something was happening back at *Northumberland*. A channel 16 distress call. Something was going on, and it was going on nearby.

The distress call came from a vessel called the MV *Saldanha*. It had a crew of 22, including 19 Filipinos, and was registered to the Marshall Islands in the north Pacific Ocean. On the bridge of the *Northumberland* the radio operator made contact. 'Can you tell me what your situation is? What's going on now?'

A hesitant voice replied. It spoke English but with a heavy accent. 'Three speedboats on the starboard side. They send a message to slow down. The mother ship is on our port side, about one and a half to two miles.'

You didn't have to be a naval expert to twig that it sounded suspicious. The officer operating the radio turned to Commander Simpson for instructions. 'Do you want them to increase speed and start manoeuvring, sir?'

More from the *Saldanha*: 'They are still approaching us, at low speed now. We'll try to keep them astern.' He didn't sound entirely confident.

The radio operator received his instructions, then relayed them: '*Saldanha*, this is Foxtrot 23. I want you to increase speed to your maximum and start manoeuvring heavily to port and starboard.'

77

This was a defensive manoeuvre. If the *Saldanha* could get up speed and then start swerving, it would create a wave and make it more difficult for the pirates – if indeed that's what they were – to approach. In the meantime, Commander Simpson ordered the Merlin, with us on board, into action. 'Send the helicopter off to that bearing.' It looked like we were about to have our first taste of piracy.

The MV *Saldanha* was 60 miles from our current position. In a Merlin helicopter in clear conditions, that takes about 12 minutes. Not a long time, but we were all aware of the need for speed. If these *were* pirates, we knew that they could board the *Saldanha* extremely quickly, and once this had been completed, there was nothing we could do about it. There was a feeling of tense expectation in the helicopter as it sped towards its target; and if it was tense for us, I couldn't help wondering what it must have been like for the crew that believed itself to be under attack.

As we crossed the water as fast as the machinery would allow, the *Saldanha* kept in constant contact with *Northumberland*, relaying its precise position. But at that distance the warship was of little practical use to the merchant vessel. It was all going to be down to the Merlin. The Marine snipers took up their positions, but I couldn't help thinking that, if it came down to it and the sniper with the AW50 had to destroy the pirates' engine blocks, these would be pretty hard shots to make, being from one unstable platform to another. I pointed this out to one of the Marines and he didn't disagree.

The minutes passed. *Saldanha* appeared as a blur on the high-definition screens when we were still eight minutes away. We were approaching from the west, and word came through that an American missile cruiser in the vicinity – the USS *Vella Gulf* – had dispatched a second helicopter from the east, which was also hurrying towards the distressed ship. For both aircraft it was a race against time. We *had* to catch the pirates in the act of taking the ship. From a distance the Merlin's cameras scanned the decks of the *Saldanha*, looking for signs of boarding. So far, nothing. But we didn't know how long that would last.

Four minutes away.

GPMG prepped and ready to go.

Update from the *Saldanha*. 'The mother ship is about three miles behind me. One fast boat together with this vessel. The other three fast boats, they run away. Maybe they are now eight, nine miles far from me.'

The skiffs were retreating. Evidently the *Saldanha*'s evasive action had deterred the supposed pirates.

The American helicopter arrived at the *Saldanha* first. It circled the vessel to assess the situation. Our pilot opened up communications with the American ship and reported back to *Northumberland*. 'Just spoke to the *Vella Gulf*, sir. Their cab's [helicopter] on top. Don't assess it as a threat. They're keeping it there to monitor the situation. He says it's more likely they'll RTB their cab shortly.'

Not a threat? Well, perhaps. But I couldn't help thinking it was unlikely that those skiffs had been closing in on the *Saldanha* just for the hell of it. The same thoughts were clearly going through Commander Simpson's head. 'I want to know when he's absolutely convinced they're fishermen, not pirates,' he instructed. As we all knew, however, telling the difference between the two is not always straightforward.

The assessment was eventually made that the retreating

skiffs were fishermen chasing tuna, but we didn't have the chance to consider how likely or unlikely that was, because just then the Merlin crew received new orders. Yet another suspicious vessel ten miles back the way we'd come. The pilot performed an about turn, leaving the *Saldanha* to go on its way while we hurried to assess the new threat. The snipers remained at their stations as I gazed at the water below.

A small flotilla of yachts came into view, boats that looked like they'd be more at home off the Côte d'Azur than in Pirate Alley. I have to admit that a part of me wondered what the hell they were doing in that part of the world; it's certainly not where I'd choose to take a yachting holiday. A skiff had been chasing them, or at least had appeared to be chasing them. But now it had backed off. Once more word came through that it was just a fishing vessel. Yet again a false alarm.

The sun was beginning to set as we returned to HMS *Northumberland*. It had been an exhausting afternoon, and a frustrating one. I'd learned a lot about the job the Royal Navy is asked to do in the Gulf of Aden. I'd come to realize that although there is a formidable military presence in that waterway, the guys are still incredibly stretched in terms of responding to the distress calls when they come in. The sheer size of the ocean they have to patrol means that the odds are stacked firmly against them.

Still, it was some small comfort that the MV *Saldanha* had been allowed to continue safely on its way.

Or had it?

6. The Pirates Strike

In the centre of HMS *Northumberland* lies the command room. It's the most heavily defended part of the ship and it is from here that the captain makes all his tactical decisions should the ship go to battle stations. And it was here that we congregated for an intelligence briefing from Sub Lieutenant Simon Henderson. 'It's believed that a majority of pirates are affiliated to clans,' he explained, 'within the northern part of Somalia. These clans give logistical support to pirates, giving enough food and supplies for vessels that are held in the detention area, and their crews. Mother ships were introduced to the piracy organizations around September last year. They allow pirates to loiter at sea, operate further out in excess of 500 nautical miles and in rougher conditions, and also hold resupplies of food, ammunition and water.'

After the briefing, I approached the sub lieutenant. I was frustrated that during our time on the ship we hadn't managed to catch up with any pirates, and I wondered if, having gathered so much detailed intelligence about them, he felt the same.

'It's extremely frustrating,' he told me. 'We have a snippet of information that in this general location there may be a pirate skiff. However, we may be two or three hundred miles away. By the time we've launched the Merlin helicopter, they're long gone. A piracy attack lasts ten or fifteen minutes.

So unfortunately, unless you're in the right place at the right time, you aren't going to catch people. It's a lot to do with luck, unfortunately.'

From my small experience so far, he was spot on. Luck hadn't been on our side. And it was about to run out for a merchant ship not a million miles from where we were at that very moment.

Pirates like to attack at dusk or at dawn, when the half-light cloaks them and they can approach their targets with less chance of being seen. In this respect they are very much like their buccaneer and corsair predecessors. As dawn broke the following day, I looked out from deck to see shoals of dolphins diving through the waves. A beautiful sight. Despite others' attempts to pollute it, this remains a very clear sea. That morning we were due to come alongside an American oiler to refuel. This vessel was absolutely vast, dwarfing even the *Northumberland*, and it was an intricate operation to pull up against it. The oiler used a rifle to fire a line over; *Northumberland* reciprocated and this continued until a network of wires existed between the two ships and they could pull themselves together. Once we were close enough, an enormous pump was winched over to us, and the ship started to refuel. The whole process took a good couple of hours. We were taking receipt of 200 tonnes of oil, after all.

What none of us knew, however, was that we were not the only vessel in the vicinity to be drawing up alongside another. As *Northumberland* had its oil thirst quenched, the crew of a merchant ship 60 miles away was coming under attack. That merchant ship went by the name of the MV *Saldanha*. The same ship we had attended the previous day on account of it being followed by skiffs that had been dismissed as fishermen chasing tuna . . .

The bridge of the *Northumberland* had no idea anything was happening until it picked up something odd on the radar. *Saldanha*, which had been doggedly plotting its course along the corridor, had now changed direction. It was no longer part of the convoy. Instead, it was heading towards the coastline of Somalia.

Commander Simpson's face was grim when he realized what was happening, and a tenseness fell upon everyone in the ship. The officer operating the radio tried to make contact: 'MV *Saldanha*, MV *Saldanha*. This is coalition warship Foxtrot 23. Channel 16. Over.'

Silence on the airwaves. *Saldanha* wasn't responding.

We couldn't hear it, but we could see it – a blip on the radar travelling off route, away from the corridor and towards the coastal town of Eyl. And if it was going to Eyl, that could mean only one thing.

Eyl is situated in the Puntland region of Somalia from which most of the pirates originate. Only a few years ago it was little more than a poor fishing town – some boats, a few shacks and a population of impoverished Somalis. All in all, not much different from the rest of the country. But Eyl has undergone a transformation, and that transformation has occurred because it is a modern-day pirate town, the lair of the people wreaking havoc in the Gulf of Aden. The shacks are still there, but they are now accompanied by signs of wealth. There are restaurants, for example, and four-by-fours driven by men in suits. The number of people engaged in actual piracy is relatively small, but a whole economy has sprung up in Eyl to service their needs.

Whenever a vessel is pirated, wealthy middlemen appear. They have new weapons and shiny cars, and you can bet your bottom dollar they didn't acquire these status symbols by honest, straightforward means. Houses are being built along the coastline surrounding Eyl – not the poor places that are the mainstay of the rest of the country, but large properties for the successful practitioners of Puntland's illegal profession.

Commander Simpson immediately changed *Northumberland*'s bearing to follow the *Saldanha*. It was eight miles away and moving steadily in a south-easterly direction. There had been no distress call from the ship, but everyone knew that her drastic change in course was not a good sign. The Merlin crew was scrambled, and I took to the air with them once again. We needed to get to the merchant vessel as quickly as possible. The bridge must have been taken, but maybe other parts of the ship hadn't. Perhaps we could help the crew with covering fire, although nobody was under the illusion that the odds were in our favour.

On the bridge, *Northumberland* continued trying to contact the vessel. 'MV *Saldanha*, MV *Saldanha*. This is coalition warship Foxtrot 23. Over.'

A deafening and very meaningful silence.

The Merlin approached. Once more, the *Saldanha* appeared on the screens in the cockpit. The bridge and the upper deck were clearly visible. No sign of anyone, or anything.

And still, nothing from the captain of the ship.

Then the radio burst into life.

It was the *Saldanha*'s captain, his accented English strangely emotionless as he updated the warship on their situation.

84

'*Saldanha* captain speaking. We are under a hostage situation. Control of the vessel is seized by pirates.'

'How many crew do you have on board?' the radio operator requested.

'We are 22. For the moment all of them OK.'

For the moment. But you don't take hostages if you're not prepared to hurt them.

Suddenly the Merlin picked up something on the *Saldanha*'s bridge. The crew reported back to *Northumberland*, 'Captain, there is a two-person visual on the bridge roof.'

The order came through to load the GPMG. 'Load gun. Roger, load gun.' The gunner had eyes on. We were one squeeze of the trigger away from an air-to-sea battle.

More info from the *Saldanha*'s captain: 'The pirates request to stay away and not to transmit any other message to them.'

Our options had been cut short. The Merlin had some powerful weaponry trained on the enemy, but it was as good as useless. Fire on the pirates and we risked two things. First, a counter-attack, using RPGs, on the helicopter. It would have been a brave move by the pirates, but then their bravery was something nobody could call into question. Second, retaliation aimed not at us but at the hostages. So far in the Gulf of Aden pirates had refrained from harming their hostages, and they knew it was in everyone's interests to keep it that way.

Commander Simpson's options were limited. He could monitor the situation, observe the *Saldanha*'s movements. But he couldn't take any military action. He couldn't board the vessel or attempt to seize it back from the pirates. The honest truth was that he could do nothing of any practical use. It was a galling moment. There we were, the Merlin hovering above the pirated vessel, *Northumberland* a handful of miles away. All that military hardware primed and ready to do its job. But in the final analysis it was worthless.

The MV *Saldanha* had just been pirated from right under our very noses. It was on its way to a known pirate haven and there wasn't a thing we could do about it.

The frustration was tangible, not just for the Marines, who had the pirates in their sights, would have liked to have taken a shot and attempted to seize the vessel, but whose hands were tied; but also for the crew as a whole. To avoid any danger to the crew, Commander Simpson ordered the Merlin to RTB immediately. The helicopter swerved.

'How you feeling?' I asked the pilot.

'I'm pissed off.'

'How frustrating is that?'

'Fucking frustrating.'

'Roger that.'

All I could do was agree with them as the crew of *Northumberland* watched the pirated *Saldanha* sail right past them, headed for the coast of Somalia.

And what of the crew of the merchant vessel? What could they expect? I could only imagine how terrified they must be. The pirates that were now swarming over their ship would be heavily armed. But in fact bloodshed would be a worst-case scenario for the pirates just as much as for the crew. They knew that as soon as they started killing or even hurting their hostages, they could expect military reprisals. Take care of them and, as they had seen time and again, they'd be given an easy ride: coalition warships would avoid boarding them in order to maintain the bloodless status quo. Moreover, the crew was the pirates' collateral. Their bargaining chips. As the *Saldanha* slipped away into the distance, I recalled the conversation I'd had before I left with the spook whose business took him into Somalia. He had explained to me that the pirates would go out of their way to protect their assets. 'If you had a car that you wanted to sell, would you go around and smash it up? No, you'd look after it – you'd clean it, you'd make sure the engine was OK, make sure it had oil and water.'

Once the *Saldanha* reached land, the pirates would make some attempt to ensure the hostages were comfortable. They have set themselves up to provide Western food in Eyl, and while the hostages would hardly be living in the lap of luxury, they could at least expect to be kept in reasonable health. That said, every part of Somalia is dangerous and unpredictable. The pirates might want to protect their assets, but that didn't mean their safety was assured. Not by any means. I wouldn't want to be in the shoes of those hostages, no matter how much pizza and Coke my captors fed me.

Saldanha did finally make it to port and, thanks to the restraint of Commander Simpson and the Marines, without anyone getting hurt. The vessel remained there for two months, supported by the infrastructure of the pirate town. It later transpired that the lead pirate went by the name of Abdirashid Ahmed. His nickname was Juqraafi – 'Geography'. Several weeks after his escapades in the Gulf of Aden, our geographical mastermind reportedly took receipt of a ransom of $1.3 million before releasing the ship and its hostages unharmed. Not a bad fee for a few minutes' work.

His original demand was for $17 million, but Juqraafi claimed that he lowered it when it became clear that the negotiations would otherwise drag on too long. This extended period of negotiation is completely normal: as soon as the pirated ships hit land, the ransom demand becomes like any other business transaction, with one side trying to keep the price up, the other doing what they can to lower it. Once the deal is done, the money can be delivered by a variety of methods.

It is believed that until recently pirates' ransoms have been transferred using an informal Islamic system called *hawala*. This system has its origins in Islamic law and has been around since at least the eighth century. It relies on a network of brokers. If a customer wishes to transfer money to somebody in another city, they give the money to one of these brokers, along with the details of the person to whom it is to be sent. The broker will contact another *hawala* broker in the recipient's city, instruct them to make the payment and then will settle the debt at a later date. Nowadays such a payment can be completed within 24 hours.

It's a simple system, but one based entirely on trust. If a sender loses his or her money, they don't have a legal leg to stand on. Moreover, *hawala* operates entirely outside the international banking system. And it's huge. According to the United Nations, somewhere between $100 billion and $300 billion is transferred through the system each year. Of this, around $15 billion enters India, $7 billion enters Pakistan, and just under a billion goes into Somalia.

Hawala is popular for a number of reasons. It's cheaper than using a bank, for a start – *hawala* brokers charge a much smaller percentage than their bank counterparts.

Modern-day pirates: not
exactly Jack Sparrow.

Pirates off the coast of Somalia hold Skipper Florent Lemacon and the
four passengers (including his wife and three-year-old son) on board the
French yacht *Tanit* to ransom. Tragically, Lemacon later took a bullet in
the head and died during a rescue attempt.

After almost 20 years of civil war, Somalia is a country ripped apart.

One in six children under the age of five suffers acute malnourishment; one in four dies before they reach this age.

Captain Lieutenant Commander Martin Simpson welcomes me on board the HMS *Northumberland* in the port of Salalah on the coast of Oman.

I take a look at the radar screen on the HMS *Northumberland*.

Searching for pirates 24/7: a constant watch is kept on the bridge.

This ship would be very difficult for pirates to board because of its high freeboard.

A vulnerable ship pumps sea water from its fire hoses to prevent pirates from boarding.

Captain Andy Morris gives his briefing before searching a suspicious vessel.

Aboard a Royal Marine RIB – rigid inflatable boat – speeding towards a suspicious skiff.

Drugs and guns are not the only cargo being transported across the Gulf of Aden. These are desperate people trying to leave a war-torn country.

Boarding the Merlin helicopter.

More unfortunate Africans risking the dangers of being smuggled across the water to Yemen.

To alleviate the boredom, the Marines are continually cleaning and stripping their weapon systems.

Decompressing in the 45-man mess, so called because, surprise surprise, 45 men live in it.

Northumberland makes contact with the pirated MV *Saldanha*.

This is a classic pirates' skiff. Fuel, water, food and the big giveaway, the 12-foot ladder.

Captain Andy Morris finds two RPG warheads on board, further proof that these guys aren't fishermen.

The pirates' skiff finally sinks as the mini-gunner looks on.

Each year, more than 100 oil workers are kidnapped by pirates in Nigeria.

The Niger Delta's maze of mangrove swamps makes it the perfect hiding place.

Robin Barry Hughes and Matthew Maguire, two British hostages who were kidnapped by pirates and held deep in the impenetrable Niger Delta.

Billy Graham was kidnapped by Nigerian pirates, held captive for 26 days without food and forced to dig his own grave.

Duncan Macnicol, a former ship's captain, takes me out into Lagos harbour, and explains how the merchant shipping vessels waiting to enter the harbour are sitting ducks: easy targets for pirates.

Hell on earth. Ajegunle is Lagos's biggest waterside slum. It's difficult to say how many people live here, but one thing's for sure – it's too many.

The slum is so polluted that you can't see the riverbank for the rubbish that is piled up by the side of the water. It was like crossing the River Styx.

One of the 17 or so chiefs of Ajegunle gives me a tour of the area and explains some of the effects piracy has had on his community.

Sonny takes me to see a damaged oil well head in Ogoniland in the heart of the Niger Delta.

A leaking deserted oil head, the cause of devastating pollution to the surrounding area.

The oil companies claim to have 'cleaned up' this area. It didn't look very clean to me.

I meet Ledum Mitee, a human rights campaigner for the Ogoni people.

Their exchange rates are often better and, most importantly, *hawala* brokers don't ask any questions. They also don't keep detailed records of individual transactions, just a running total of the amount owed by one broker to another. It's easy to use the *hawala* system to make anonymous payments that are difficult to trace. Pay someone by *hawala* and there's no paper trail. As such, it has often been used to finance terrorism and other illegal activites – after the 11 September attacks the United States urged greater regulations of *hawala* operators.

It is thought that some pirates in Puntland purchase weapons by sending money via *hawala* to dealers in Mogadishu. It also seems likely, as there are no banks or Western Union offices that can transfer money in and out of Somalia, that the system has been used in some instances to arrange payment of pirates' ransoms. But it is reported that the ransoms eventually grew too big for even the *hawala* system to cope with. Rumours now abound – unsubstantiated, it should be said – that teams of ex-special forces personnel are sometimes engaged to perform a cash dump onto the deck of the ship in question. I've also been told that money is simply transferred from one bank account to another in, for example, the City of London. That made me wonder just who was behind these operations, and it made me realize that the people committing these acts of piracy are nothing if not savvy.

Juqraafi the pirate has gone on record as saying that the pirates have well-organized systems for divvying up the loot. They generally have a 'financier' who sponsors them – he gets 30 per cent. The pirates themselves get 50 per cent. The remaining 20 per cent is divided out among the community and those who have helped the pirates on shore in some way – including corrupt officials who expect bribes whenever a ship is successfully taken.

How true pirates' claims of Robin Hood-like generosity are, it's impossible to say. They certainly have support among particular sections of the population, but in a part of the world that remains grindingly poor there seems little doubt that the people who benefit the most from these crimes are the pirates themselves and the Mr Bigs that support them.

Back on HMS *Northumberland*, none of us knew how long the *Saldanha* would remain in port, or whether the crew would come to any harm in the lawless town of Eyl. There wasn't a man or woman on our ship that didn't feel the frustration keenly. There was nothing anybody could do about the pirated vessel itself, but we knew that the pirates had to have gained access to the merchant ship somehow, and there had been no sign of any skiffs attached to the *Saldanha*. So it was that Merlin set off once again. Its mission this time was to scour the seas for a mother ship or any skiffs floating in the vicinity.

It didn't take long for the Merlin to pick up a faint echo on the radar in the area of ocean where the *Saldanha* was pirated. The Fleet Protection Group immediately manned the RIBs and I joined them as they sped through the waves on the bearing the helicopter had indicated. The Marines expected it to be a skiff, and they weren't disappointed: within minutes, we came across a long, solitary vessel, floating innocuously. We approached with caution, not knowing if the skiff was booby-trapped, and as Captain Andy Morris and Sergeant Macaffer gingerly boarded the empty vessel, that caution doubled. It would only take a primed hand grenade sitting under an RPG and suddenly we'd be swimming with the fishes.

The skiff was battered, old and very far from glamorous, but it contained everything necessary to carry out an act of piracy. Two Yamaha outboard motors – big enough to allow the vessel to catch up with a merchant ship – and plenty of canisters of fuel to power them, plus a 12-foot ladder, long enough to board most low-freeboard vessels. In addition, the Marines found plenty of items on board which suggested that the pirates hadn't wanted to lose this skiff. There were wrapped-up wads of Somali cash – too much for any fisherman. There were clothes and shoes – the pirates must have boarded barefoot, but in poor countries like Somalia shoes are important, so they definitely wouldn't have left them there on purpose. We found two RPG warheads, but no launcher. You wouldn't have the warheads without the launcher, which meant they must have boarded with it; and they wouldn't have boarded with a launcher and no warhead – they probably had several with them. There were shell casings from an AK-47 lying in the hull of the boat. It was impossible to say when they had been fired; all we knew was that they *had* been fired, and that the pirates were more than likely armed with assault rifles. There was the obligatory camel meat, and a large bunch of a green plant that looked a bit like basil. This was khat, an amphetamine-like stimulant indigenous to East Africa and the Arabian peninsula. It's illegal in Somalia but widely available, and it's said to be a particular favourite of the pirates. Khat keeps you awake, suppresses your appetite and gives you an addictive high. Some people chew the leaves, others the stalk, mashing it to a paste in their mouth which they keep there for a long time, sucking out all the juices before spitting it out again when it's served its purpose.

We also found an expensive sea compass that they wouldn't have wanted to lose and, bizarrely, a blue strap with the word 'Arsenal' embroidered on it. Clearly our men liked the Gunners as well as their guns. Our suspicions that the skiff had been lost rather than abandoned were confirmed when the Marines located, tied to the end of the boat, a frayed piece of rope that had clearly once been attached to something but had then snapped. It was impossible to ascertain how many people had been on this skiff and subsequently boarded the *Saldanha*; indeed, there might well have been two skiffs, with the second speeding back to some mother ship nearby, ready to go shopping again if a suitable target crossed its path. All we could say for sure was that this skiff had once been tied to something – most probably the merchant vessel itself – and that it belonged not to fishermen, but to pirates.

Captain Andy Morris jettisoned the RPG warheads over the side of the skiff. They sank without trace and it was good to know that, submerged in 2,500 feet of water, they were now harmless. But an unmanned floating skiff remained a hazard to navigation, so back on the bridge of HMS *Northumberland* the captain received permission to destroy the vessel. It was up to the Marines to bring the skiff within range of the frigate's guns, so they attached a rope and used their RIBs to bring it in. I made the return journey in the skiff. In fact, I insisted on it. I might have missed out on meeting a pirate, but I wanted at least to ride in his boat.

Once the Marines and I were safely back on board *Northumberland*, the skiff was set adrift. But it wouldn't sail for long. Already the ship's gunners had it in their sights, and as soon as the skiff was a safe distance away, one of them opened up with a Minigun, a multi-barrel machine gun that fires 7.62 mm rounds at a rate of over 3,000 a minute. The ocean around the skiff was peppered with little explosions, and as the rounds slammed into the skiff itself, the fuel canisters ignited and it burst into flame. A thick black plume of smoke billowed up from it, and still the rounds from the Minigun came, the noise from the weapon thundering into the air around us. The skiff still wasn't sinking, so the captain ordered the larger 30 mm Oerlikon guns on it.

It took a lot of firepower to sink that skiff. More than I would have expected. Or maybe the gunner was just taking out his frustrations on that tiny vessel, a lone symbol of the opportunity *Northumberland* had just narrowly missed to do what it had been put in the Gulf of Aden to do and catch a team of pirates. I wouldn't have blamed him. As the skiff burned and sank, all we could do was reflect on the fact that combating piracy off the coast of Somalia is a bit like finding a needle in a haystack. If you're not in the right place at the right time, you simply don't stand a chance.

Our time on board the Royal Navy frigate was coming to a close. HMS *Northumberland* was on a bearing towards the port of Djibouti, and it was here that we were to disembark. Djibouti is a tiny country on the northern border of Somalia: a population of half a million, a fifth of whom live below the poverty line. Like Somalia, it has come through a period of civil war, but Djibouti, at least, has a functioning government. It's not exactly a safe haven, but in this part of the world all things are relative, and it's a hell of a sight safer than Eyl, where at that moment the MV *Saldanha* was taking its place alongside 16 other pirated vessels. In addition to its crew, there were also 292 other hostages in that pirate haven.

It was disappointing that during my time on board *Northumberland* we had not managed to catch up with a pirate. I'd learned a lot about the difficulties the British navy and others face in their struggle against this seaborne menace. I'd seen at first hand just how hard it is to catch pirates, and witnessed the frustration of the men and women of the Royal Navy at how little they could do. At the same time, I could understand how careful the coalition warships in the Gulf of Aden have to be. Just a couple of months previously an Indian frigate by the name of INS *Tabar* had destroyed a deep-sea trawler which they claimed was a pirate arsenal, full to the brim with supplies of weapons and ammo. Unfortunately, they were wrong. It was in fact a Thai fishing boat that had been hijacked, which still contained the entire crew, tied up below decks. Only one of them was ever found alive. A cautionary tale of the dangers involved in using your superior military strength. Later in my investigation I met a group of former Marines and Paras. Ordinarily, they would be plying their trade as private security guards in hot spots like Iraq, but they explained to me that their livelihoods had been taken by younger lads prepared to do the same job for a lot less money. And so they had diversified, offering themselves up to merchant vessels who wanted a bit of extra insurance. These guys weren't allowed to take any weapons on board ship with them, so they had to make do with whatever they might find on a merchant vessel – fire extinguishers, hammers and the wherewithal to make Molotov cocktails. Their hands were tied, but maybe it was for the best, as later events in the Gulf of Aden would demonstrate the human cost of taking the fight to the pirates with genuine weapons.

But that was in the future. For now, I had made some good friends on the *Northumberland*, but what I really wanted to do had so far eluded me: to speak to a pirate, and to find out straight from the horse's mouth what drives them to these crimes on the high seas. Is it poverty? Is it organized crime? Is it sheer opportunism? Or is it a mixture of all three? As we said goodbye to the friends we had made on board ship, I realized that I still had a lot more to learn. What I didn't know was that my next trip, to the waters of a country many hundreds of miles from Somalia, would show me a very different side to the menace of international piracy.

PART 2
The Bight of Benin

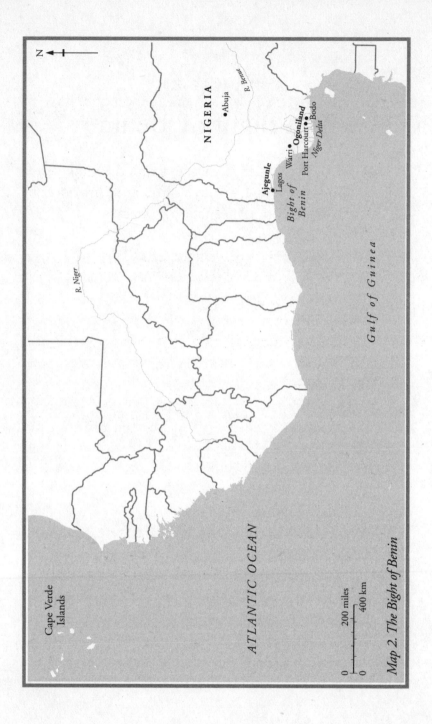

Map 2. The Bight of Benin

7. Chop-chop

There's an old sea shanty, dating from the nineteenth century, about the area I was to visit next in my quest to discover the truth about international piracy.

> Beware, beware the Bight of Benin
> There's one that comes out for forty goes in.

That cheerful little jingle was inspired by the risk of malaria to anyone venturing into that part of the world, and it's true that the illness is more of a threat in this part of Africa than almost anywhere else. But the Bight's inhospitable nature was not limited to deadly mosquitoes. It was famously a hub of the slave trade; indeed this stretch of land along the western coast of Africa was known as the Slave Coast, and as such it was a busy waterway for ships full of misery.

Nowadays, boats that travel through these waters have different cargos, some legal, some not. The Gulf of Guinea, which comprises the Bight of Benin, the neighbouring Bight of Bonny and the coastlines of the 11 countries that lie between Ghana and Angola, is a major hub for narcotics trafficking. In recent years significant quantities of high-grade cocaine have been seized in these waters because it is part of the drug-trade triangular route between the Cape Verde Islands, the Canary Islands and Madeira.

As well as being part of a drug route, since the late 1990s

the area has consistently ranked as one of the top piracy hot spots worldwide. In the two years between 2002 and 2004 there were more pirate attacks in the Gulf of Guinea than in the rest of African waters put together. Today, it is officially the world's second-biggest piracy hot spot after Somalia, but that statistic doesn't tell the whole story. A large number of pirate attacks in the Gulf go unreported. After all, if someone nicks your stash of coke, you're hardly likely to go moaning to the authorities. And if you're a fisherman whose small boat has been boarded, all your money pinched and then you've been thrown overboard and left to your own luck – well, the chances are you're not going to survive long enough to report the incident. No one knows how many ships are currently being pirated here, but it is thought the Gulf could easily knock Somalia off the top spot.

The Gulf of Guinea extends for 3,400 miles. That's about the same size as the Gulf of Mexico and in an area of coastline that size, there's bound to be bits that are less safe than others. One country along the Gulf has the dubious honour of playing host to the majority of pirate attacks in the area. That country is Nigeria, and its piracy problem is escalating. Big time. In 2003 there were four reported attacks; in 2008 there were 107. The Nigerian Trawler Owners' Association reckoned that in 2006 half of all fishing vessels in Nigerian waters had been pirated. The International Transport Workers' Federation, which represents workers in 148 different countries, has branded Nigeria's waters a war zone.

Nigerian pirates are different from Somali pirates in one important respect: they kill people. This hasn't always been the case – until a few years ago they principally targeted cash, valuables and shipping gear. Not any more. Violence is a regular occurrence, and so are killings. In one week alone, not long before I travelled to Nigeria, there were 20 attacks on ships and 10 people killed.

And I don't mind admitting that I didn't much like the sound of those odds.

Nigeria's a long way from home. But I didn't even have to leave Britain in order to discover that the effects of the country's piracy problem reached much further than the African coastline. Instead I prepared to meet the Maguire family from the Wirral. Anxious times for anxious people, as I found out when I spoke to Bernard Maguire, whose son Matthew was one of a group of British oil-rig workers who had been on a boat moored at Port Harcourt, the capital of Nigeria's Rivers State. Matthew is an electrician by trade but wasn't making the money he needed, so he retrained as a diver. Divers are important to the oil industry, which needs them to work on underwater drilling, inspecting pipes or fixing oil derricks. Diving can be well paid, and Matthew was on a ship waiting to be transported to an oil platform further out to sea so that he could earn a living for himself and his family.

Unfortunately, things didn't quite go according to plan. The ship was hijacked by 8 to 10 pirates, and 27 crew members originating from a variety of countries were forced into a smaller vessel and onto land. This area of Nigeria is characterized by a vast network of waterways and inlets. The pirates moved their hostages into a smaller speedboat still, and then ferried them to a nearby village.

Over the next few days most of the hostages were released, and each time someone was released, the pirates moved somewhere else along these complex waterways so they couldn't be tracked down. First the pirates let the Nigerian nationals go, then the various foreign nationals until they had whittled it down to their two British captives. Matthew Maguire and Robin Barry Hughes, captain of the pirated ship, were retained. It turned out that the pirates specifically wanted British hostages, for reasons I would come to understand once I got to Nigeria. The pirates took their hostages deep into the Niger Delta – 27,000 square miles of intricate, intertwined waterways that cover nearly a tenth of Nigeria's land mass. There was some attempt by the authorities to locate them, but it was an impossible task. Hole yourself away in the Niger Delta and nobody is ever going to find you . . .

All this had happened some five months previously. Since that time neither man's family had heard from him. Matthew Maguire had a wife and three young children back home, and his father's face spoke eloquently about his worry as I sat down to talk to him. Word had reached him that one of the two hostages was seriously ill, but they didn't know which one. I could only imagine the worry the family must have been feeling. 'It's little things of a night,' he told me, trying to put a brave face on it, but not entirely succeeding, 'when you're trying to go to sleep, or you wake up early because you're thinking about the conditions he's kept in. Stupid things like shower, clothes, what food is he eating, where's he sleeping.' All the minutiae of day-to-day living, the things parents are hard-wired to worry about, no matter that their son was grown up with children of his own. Stupid things? They didn't sound stupid to me at all, especially knowing what I knew about Nigerian pirates' readiness to kill their hostages.

The question was, why had Matthew Maguire and Robin Barry Hughes been taken? Was this an opportunist attack like the one I had witnessed in the Gulf of Aden? Were the pirates looking for a sizeable monetary ransom in return for their assets? Or was there something else going on here? In order to work out the reasons for Matthew Maguire's kidnapping, I would have to learn more about the precarious political situation in Nigeria. As had been the case in the Gulf of Aden, in order to understand what was occurring on the water, I would need to gain a better grasp of what was happening on land.

The kidnapping of Matthew Maguire and Robin Barry Hughes was by no means a one-off. Until recently Nigeria was the world's eighth-biggest oil producer. Where there's oil, there are oil companies – huge multinational corporations who import workers with the expertise necessary to pump black gold from deep under the earth from around the world. In Nigeria there are an estimated 20,000 of them. These oil workers are well paid for their time and professionalism, but their rewards come at a price. Each year more than a hundred are kidnapped by pirates. If I was going to find out why this was happening, I would have to go straight to the centre of the problem. So it was that I boarded a plane for Lagos. It was the first time I had travelled to this part of Africa, and as I took to the skies I was more than a little apprehensive about what it was I would find when I got there.

In 2003 the respected magazine *New Scientist* published a survey which claimed to rank more than 65 countries in order of happiness. I don't know how you can measure happiness but Nigeria, to the surprise of many, came top. The happiest country in the world. Maybe it is. It certainly has the raw materials for happiness: sandy beaches, spectacular tropical forests, magnificent waterfalls and, perhaps most importantly, enough oil to make it one of the richest, most affluent countries on earth. You would think that the inhabitants of such a country would be very happy indeed.

But there's a flip side. Nigeria might be oil rich and beautiful, but it has some of the worst social indicators in the world. One in five children dies before the age of five; 12 million do not get to go to school; there are nearly 2 million Aids orphans; more than half the population lives below the poverty line. Life expectancy at birth is 47. Per capita income is $1,400 – that's not as bad as Somalia, but it isn't far off. Walk almost anywhere in Nigeria and you can guarantee that someone will come up and ask you for 'chop-chop' – money for food. Take a camera out, and someone will approach you, demanding to see your papers and asking for chop-chop. A lot of them are just trying it on, but plenty of Nigerians are genuinely hungry. Far be it for me to say whether these statistics should be a fly in the ointment for the Nigerian people, but I think they might take the smile off *my* face.

The Nigerians themselves have a joke. Jesus looks down from heaven and he says to God, 'Father, look at that country. They have so much. Why did you give them all this: the oil, those natural resources, the fertile soil, the beautiful landscape?' God smiles and winks at Jesus. 'Just wait,' he says, 'until you see what sort of *people* I'm going to give them.'

Perhaps the Nigerians do themselves an injustice. In my

time in their country I met some genuinely friendly, good people. But there's no way of denying that Nigeria has its fair share of rotten apples. Anyone with an email account will have received mail from scam artists claiming to be rich Nigerians, and the famous 419 scam originated in Nigeria. So called because number 419 is the article of the Nigerian criminal code pertaining to fraud, this scam involves a letter or email claiming to be from a Nigerian citizen who knows the whereabouts of a large sum of money – in the bank account of a deposed leader perhaps, or belonging to a terminally ill person with no friends or relatives. A good scammer will make some effort to ensure that the story stands up to scrutiny, so if someone decides to investigate, they don't fall at the first hurdle. The recipient of the letter – or 'investor' – is offered a substantial chunk of that money if they 'assist' the scammer in retrieving this money. If the investor bites, they are sent a load of official-looking documentation; sometimes they are asked to travel all the way to Nigeria. However the scam unfolds, you can bet your bottom dollar that at some point in the proceedings they'll be asked for money – most often to pay a tax or a bribe. And the moment they hand over any money, of course, the scammer disappears.

It might sound like a pretty obvious swindle to you and me, but if a few million such emails are sent out, it only takes a small percentage to fall for it and the exercise is made worthwhile. And worthwhile it certainly is: in Lagos, 419 scammers have proper business premises. They make money doing it. Walk around Lagos and you'll see houses and cars with the number 419 marked on them. That means, don't try to buy this house or this car: someone's already tried to do it and it doesn't really belong to the person pretending to own it.

It would be grossly unfair to paint all Nigerians with this brush, but the point is that corruption is commonplace. Every petty official will ask you for chop-chop; even the police will demand it. This corruption goes all the way up to the highest echelons of the government and, as I would find out, it's a major cause of the piracy that I was here to investigate.

Nigeria is a troubled country with a troubled history. Like so many African states, it has a history of colonization, independence and bloody civil war. The Portuguese were the first Europeans to reach the Nigerian coast, and they named the port of Lagos after the town of the same name in the Algarve. (It means 'lagoon'.) This was in the late fifteenth century, and in the 400 years that followed Nigeria became a hub of the slave trade, with millions of its people being traded, principally to the Americas but also elsewhere round the world.

The British rolled up in the nineteenth century, just after the Napoleonic wars. On 1 January 1901 the whole of Nigeria became a British protectorate, with Britain governing by 'indirect rule' through local leaders. In keeping with Britain's colonial past, the slave trade was, almost unbelievably, not banned in Nigeria until 1936. By the middle of the century, a huge wave of anti-colonial feeling was sweeping over Africa. Nigeria was no exception. Despite the fact that the country was divided into more than 200 separate tribes, there was an increase in nationalistic feeling and demands for independence became frequent. Nigeria finally gained independence in 1960, just two years after the first barrels of Nigerian crude oil left the country destined for the world market.

The first Nigerian administration – a coalition government – managed six years of power before the prime minister, the splendidly named Sir Abubakar Tafawa Balewa, was killed in a coup. There followed many years of political strife, corruption and military coups, some bloodless, others distinctly bloody. There was a three-year civil war during which a million Nigerians were killed. But throughout all this one thing kept Nigeria very firmly on the map and in the minds of major powers around the world.

Oil. Because Nigeria had, and has, a hell of a lot of it.

In the 1970s Nigeria joined OPEC – the Organization of Petroleum Exporting Countries. The densely populated Niger Delta region produced billions of dollars' worth of oil and attracted oil workers from around the world. In 1983 the government expelled over a million foreigners – mostly Ghanaians – on the basis that their visas had expired and they were taking jobs from Nigerians. It was a popular move, but of course it didn't stop people drilling for oil.

In 1991 the capital city of Nigeria was moved from Lagos on the coast to Abuja in the middle of the country. The reasons for moving the capital were numerous: Abuja was deemed to be located in territory neutral to the many tribes and clans of the country; Lagos was overcrowded and sprawling; and Lagos suffered, politically speaking, from its geographical position. It is made up of a number of islands separated by creeks, lagoons and waterways – a complicated, labyrinthine network. The main islands are connected by bridges, but are easy to defend if they're taken over in a coup. There had been so many of these since Nigeria's independence that successive governments, frightened of being deposed in the same way that they themselves had seized power, felt the need to move the capital somewhere a little more secure. Hence Abuja, which I'm told is a fantastic place with expensive buildings and manicured lawns, although you can only live there if you're in the government, the oil business or the service industries.

Truth was, however, it didn't matter how well manicured the lawns of Abuja were; from the point of view of my investigation into pirates, it was of no interest. Lagos, however – the dirty, sprawling, impoverished, busy, dirty lagoon town – was a different matter.

Lagos is the fastest-growing city on the planet. It's certainly the most chaotic I've ever been to. In the 1950s it had a population of about 250,000 people. Today, depending on who you talk to, the population is somewhere between 9 million and 18 million. It may no longer be Nigeria's capital, but it's by far the country's biggest city. Like many expanding cities, it faces certain challenges: unemployment, crime, corruption and pollution to name a few. The poverty that blights Nigeria is at its peak here: many people (though not all) live on a pittance; it has been known for armed criminals to have shoot-outs with the police in the busy streets of the city.

Now, though, it has a new problem to deal with. That problem is piracy.

Lagos is West Africa's principal and busiest port. Seventy-five per cent of all the country's goods arrive there by sea. That means a lot of shipping and, as I'd already seen, where there's lots of ships, there's lots of pirates. It was Lagos, therefore, that would be my first port of call in my attempt to hunt down the dangerous pirates of Nigeria.

Lagos is the busiest, most congested city I've ever seen. Traffic jams – or, as the Nigerians have it, 'go-slows' – sit motionless in the searing heat, the air is thick with humidity and petrol fumes and people swarm around you in their thousands. One guidebook describes it as 'chaos theory made flesh and concrete'. Elevated motorways surround the city, the ever-present go-slows on top, tin shacks underneath. I can't begin to describe how hot it is – sweat pours from your face, your eyes, and your clothes are constantly soaked. The streets are strewn with litter and the people stride around with a swaggering kind of purpose. Lagos has expanded because people come here to make money, and everyone seems to be hustling something. Millions don't succeed: you see poverty on the street corners, but I was also very aware of the divide between the haves and the have-nots. There are some very rich people in Lagos, and an expat community with its oil money and yacht clubs. As I'd seen in other parts of the world, that's never a good mix. Even though there's an expat community, white people still stick out like a sore thumb. Arrive at the port of Lagos and you can be in no doubt that you're in the heart of black Africa.

There was no luxurious accommodation for this Western film crew when we arrived in West Africa. Far from it. Our hotel, run by Christian Lebanese, was to put it mildly not nice. No concierge at the door; instead, there were grim-faced guards armed with the ubiquitous AK-47s. You only have that for one reason: because there are people out there who want to come into your hotel and steal everything you've got. The place was full of brass – prostitutes coming in and out to service the needs of the hotel's fluid population. Despite all this, there were plenty of Western faces around. Nigeria might be a tense place, but the prospect of a quick buck was enough to embolden people. A lot of these people get robbed, particularly to and from the airport and particularly if they're not with the right people (it's very rare that you see an *oyibo* – a white man – in a car by himself). But still they come.

I was doing my opening piece to camera when we came up against the difficulties of getting things done in Nigeria. I walked towards the place I'd left Will the cameraman and Kiff the sound man, unable to see them through the crowd of locals. Like all white people, we stood out, but we stood out more than most because Kiff had lost his right arm in an accident – instead of a hand he had metal pincers. Suddenly I realized the guys weren't there. I looked around. Nothing but a sea of black faces, so I used my mobile phone to call Will.

'Will, where are you?'

He almost managed to sound sheepish. 'We've been arrested,' he said.

'Arrested? Who by?'

'The port authority. For filming without permission.'

I couldn't believe what I was hearing – Will hadn't even been pointing his camera at the port. It seems that didn't matter. Day one of shooting and our camera crew had been nicked. It took ages to sort everything out, and in the end we only managed to do so by a pretty unconventional method. The guy who ran the port authority split his time between the UK and Lagos. As a result, it turned out that he was a fan. In return for a photograph with me that he could put on the Internet and a little bit of a bung, he agreed to help release Will and Kiff and give us permission to film in the port. Chop-chop, snap snap, job done. The boss man was happy and we had what we wanted, but I couldn't help wondering what would have happened if our soap opera-loving official *hadn't* recognized my face . . .

My first meeting in Nigeria was with Duncan Macnicol, a former ship's captain who now works as a shipping agent across West Africa, helping shipping operators navigate their way through the mountains of red tape, inefficiency and corruption that go with trying to get a vessel into the port of Lagos. He had lived and worked in Lagos for nearly 20 years and had promised to show me some footage of a very recent pirate attack. The captain of the targeted vessel had taken the footage from the bridge wing. It was grainy and unprofessional, but that didn't matter: you could easily make out what was going on. The pirates were using what had once been a lifeboat from a ship. I watched as the boat approached from the starboard side of the vessel. It circled round as the pirates fired heavy-calibre and automatic weapons towards the ship. You could see the flashes from the guns and hear the crack as the ammo slammed against its target. It was a violent display, full of intent and, I suppose, bravado. They clearly meant business, and you wouldn't want to be at the receiving end of an attack like that.

Duncan explained to me that piracy was on the increase in Nigeria, and the reason for this was two-fold. First, there was what was known as the Niger Delta problem. This is a political dispute which has led, among other things, to pirates attacking oil tankers in the Delta region. Second, he explained, there are so many merchant vessels lying offshore at Lagos that they are sitting ducks, easy targets for anyone of a piratical bent to hit and make a quick buck. It was the Niger Delta problem that would become the focus of my investigation into piracy in Nigeria. But before I followed that lead Duncan offered to take me out into Lagos harbour, just so I could see what he meant when he described the merchant ships out there as sitting ducks.

8. The Victims

Go-slows aren't limited to the roads of Lagos. Its port plays host to them too. The vessels might not be crunched up against each other in the same way the cars are; there may not be the shouting and the frenzy. But make no mistake about it: trying to unload your goods in Lagos means joining the mother of all traffic jams.

Extraordinary bureaucracy and a crumbling and corrupt infrastructure mean that nothing can happen at anything other than a creeping pace. To get a ship into the port of Rotterdam, which is the largest in Europe, takes something of the order of three pieces of paper. Unless anything unusual happens, you're in and out. To get a ship into Lagos harbour takes more like 70. There are layers and layers of needless bureaucracy and corruption which line the pockets of those administering the backhanders and the chop-chop and which make unloading goods a painfully slow – and potentially dangerous – occupation. At any one time there will be up to 100 ships waiting offshore to ditch their cargos. The area in which they wait is known as the quarantine anchorage, and it was around this area that I travelled with Duncan in a small boat dwarfed by the huge vessels that were laid up here.

Immobile. Valuable. Huge chunks of metal dotted around in the ocean, some of them impressive, others barely seaworthy. Ships can remain in the quarantine anchorage for many weeks. I couldn't help notice three ladies climbing the ladder of a ship. Duncan told me they were local prostitutes that did the rounds of the merchant vessels to service the needs of homesick sailors. Supply and demand . . .

I couldn't count how many ships there were, but it was absolutely clear to me that Duncan was right. The vessels I had seen in the Gulf of Aden had at least been able to perform evasive manoeuvres, could pump jets of water at attackers and had warships such as HMS *Northumberland* to patrol the waters – and still they got pirated with relative ease. These vessels had none of this. They *were* sitting ducks, clearly vulnerable to being pirated at any moment. Indeed, just four days previously, a chemical tanker had been boarded by pirates, who had beaten up the crew, stolen their money and ripped out the radio communications system, presumably so that their victims could not raise the alarm until the pirates were safely away.

We floated around the base of a vessel called the *Princess Alice*, registered in Panama. It was a long way from home, and as Duncan explained was particularly vulnerable by virtue of its fairly low freeboard. It wouldn't be too taxing to put a ladder up the side, or use a grappling hook to board the vessel. My guide explained that most attacks happen at night, the pirates using the cover of darkness to approach the ships unseen and go about their business. The smaller ships were easier to hit, he told me, because they wouldn't necessarily have 24-hour watches, and some of the bigger ships took the precaution of waiting much further out to sea, some of them not even anchored so that they could drift up and down and make it just a little bit more difficult for the pirates.

As we continued to tour the quarantine anchorage, people looked down on us from the decks of their ships. They could see the cameras we had trained on them, and I could tell that many of them were extremely edgy about that. They didn't like being filmed. They didn't like anyone taking an interest in them. I couldn't say why, but equally I couldn't help reminding myself that transporting goods by sea is a line of business that offers more opportunity for criminality than almost any other. Just because some of these ships were vulnerable to pirate attacks, that didn't mean they were entirely on the straight and narrow themselves.

I asked Duncan why it was that Nigeria imported so much. Why didn't it have any kind of manufacturing industry? He explained that it was all down to oil. When the country discovered that it was oil rich, it also discovered that it was easier to earn money from that industry than any other. 'They let the farms go,' he told me. 'They let the plantations go. In the end the Nigerians *had* to import all these goods because they couldn't produce them themselves, and they had the money to do it.' And yet, if the country was so rich, why were its people so poor? It was an important question, and one that I would have answered for me over the next few days.

As part of Duncan's guided tour of Lagos, he took us to a yacht club situated on a nearby peninsula. Drinks at the club. It sounded glamorous, but in fact the building looked like it had been built in the 1970s and was now cracking up. It felt more like an old comprehensive school than a glamorous hangout for the beautiful people. The yacht club is by a stretch of water where a river joins the ocean. You can see the brown water and the blue water mixing with each other, and they cause a wave where they meet. As the roads are so congested in Lagos, people also use boats to get around, navigating the lagoons and waterways as a means of getting from A to B. As we sat outside with our very welcome cold drinks looking out over the bustle of the water, we noticed one particular boat. It had the appearance of an old lifeboat with an outboard motor but was in fact a taxi, ferrying people round the waterways of Lagos. There must have been about 15 passengers, all of them heavily laden down with bags and belongings.

We watched it from a distance. And then, as it approached us and the fast current where the river and ocean met, it suddenly flipped over.

The boat was sinking; a lot of the passengers were struggling. The reaction from the locals was immediate and impressive. Men jumped into the water from surrounding boats and rescued all the people. A crowd of kids also jumped in. Some of them dived underneath the boat, pushing it back up; others started bailing out water quicker than it could leak into the hull so that finally it rose, phoenix-like, and righted itself. Some people then tinkered around with the engine – everything was working as it should – so the passengers got back into their taxi and off it went.

That little incident seemed to me to say a lot about Africa. If it had happened on the Thames, it would be front-page news for a week. In Nigeria they just get on with it. Far worse things happen in that part of the world, so they don't have the inclination to hang about wringing their hands. I was also struck by how ready everybody was to help out. Nigeria certainly has a criminal underbelly, but while I was there I also saw such moments of selfless kindness that put the Nigerian people in an altogether better light. In Afghan-istan I had observed how the Afghan people were brilliant at recycling and reusing things; the same was true of Nigeria. Everyone talks about how bad the Third World is at recy-cling – and as I was soon to find out, Nigeria had more than its fair share of environmental problems. But the truth is that in poor places nobody *wants* to throw anything away if it can be fixed and has some use. There was no way anyone was going to let that boat sink. It would be patched up, put to work and no doubt earn a living for its owner for a good few years to come. I think our disposable society could learn a lot from that.

It is not just merchant shipping that is under threat from piracy. Unlike the pirates of Somalia, Nigerian pirates don't just go for big game; they hit the tiddlers too. Lagos has – or at least it had – a large deep-sea fishing fleet, but as I explored the main fishing port I saw that a large number of the trawl-ers had been tied up and left to rust. The world was in the middle of an economic downturn at the time, but this wasn't an economic problem. It was a criminal one. Over the last few years pirate attacks on fishermen in these waters had increased three-fold. Many of these attacks go unreported, and as they don't have much in the way of wider ramifica-tions for the international community, the world's press has pretty well ignored the issue. One report, though, tells of an attack in which the pirates boarded a ship at 1.30 a.m., shot the ship's cook through the belly and then proceeded to eat the food that he had prepared earlier while he lay dying in agony, before looting the ship of all the money and goods they could find, including the captain's shoes. (I told you shoes were important in poor parts of the world.) The captain went on record as saying, 'There were attacks before, but it's the worst now. Formerly we had hijackings and they would steal everything, but now they attack and they are shooting and taking lives.'

The statistics show this to be true: over the past four years, 298 fisherman had lost their lives to pirates. That's more than one a week.

In response to the problem, the Nigerian Trawler Owners' Association recalled all its ships into port and led a series of demonstrations to raise awareness – in 2008 they even blockaded Lagos itself. 'The pirates have established a republic in a republic,' they announced. 'They have their own commander in chief. You have to pay to be allowed to fish. You will be given their flag before you are allowed to fish. They are a country of their own.'

The threat from pirates was so immediate and acute that we could find nobody willing to talk to us on the record about it. One man, though, agreed to be interviewed on the strict proviso that we didn't reveal his identity. He ran a fleet of 69 vessels operating out of the port of Lagos – shrimping boats, there to take advantage of the fact that the waters around Nigeria supply some of the best and most abundant shellfish in the world. His business, and the livelihoods of the men he employed, was being crippled by the effects of these attacks.

I asked him how often his 69 vessels came into contact with pirates.

'It's more or less a daily affair,' he told me.

So when was the last time one of his vessels was attacked?

'This week I've had twelve.'

Sounded more than daily to me. I wondered what had happened to the crews of these trawlers.

'They've beaten them up. I've had four or five of them hospitalized. You see, the people come on board with guns, or they come shooting. Whether they do anything to you or not, *they* are traumatized and *I* am traumatized.' Having been shot at a few times myself, I could well believe it. 'I am scared to send off my vessels,' he continued. 'I normally don't have so many vessels in port.'

It was true. His trawlers were lined up in the water, neat and useless. Elsewhere in the port I had seen a substantial number of vessels in a state of run-down disrepair, now just rusting hulls. Some of them had been left to rot in the saltwater; others had been plundered for scrap and spare parts. It was clear that no one was ever going to move these boats from the port of Lagos. They'd just be left to sink into the harbour. I couldn't help wondering if, thanks to the attention of the pirates, this was the fate that awaited my interviewee's fleet.

I wanted to know if he thought the pirates attacking his ship were just opportunist criminals, or if they were a bit more organized than that. He shook his head. 'They come in boats with bulletproof vests.'

Body armour?

'Yeah, body armour. They've got enough fuel supply to remain 40 miles offshore.'

That sounded to me like a gang that knew what it was doing.

'No place is safe,' the trawler owner told me. He explained that when a trawler is travelling with its nets down, it moves very slowly – around two and a half knots – and its freeboard is only about eight feet high. 'You're a sitting duck.'

It wasn't the first time I'd heard that phrase used in Lagos, and I was beginning to understand just what a problem piracy was in this town.

I'd heard a lot *about* pirates, but I was still no closer to speaking to one. Trouble was, I wasn't the only person who wanted to catch up with these people – who, for good reasons, didn't want to be caught up with. Even more problematically, they have a very good place to hide. The maze of waterways that surrounds Lagos is the perfect environment for them. It's huge, complicated and nigh-on impossible to police. Finding pirates among the labyrinth of backwaters and miles of open ocean was not an easy task for the authorities, and it wasn't going to be an easy task for us.

We hadn't yet got an in with a pirate, but we had received word that one of their victims was willing to talk to us. His name was Billy Graham (no relation), an American who had been in the oil business since 1991. He made his living working for a company that supplied machinery to oil platforms off the Nigerian coast. During the working week he and his colleagues lived in a gated community near the port. Not luxurious exactly, but a far cry from the pronounced poverty that exists literally just over the wall. In their downtime, however, they travelled up to a beach residence, where they could chill out away from the bustle and the dirt of Lagos.

It was a hot, uncomfortable journey of about four hours up into the network of channels behind Lagos. As we travelled, I noticed a lot of what are known as sand barges. These are long, thin boats, very low in the water. Men dive from these boats with an empty bucket, down to the bottom, where they fill their bucket with sand and bring it back to the surface. There's a global demand for sand, and it has to be collected somehow. These men are out there from dawn till dusk. That's what I call a tough way to make a living. If I ever find myself moaning about my day, I think of the sand barges of Nigeria and it puts things in perspective.

Our destination was a white enclave with a number of weekend residences of the type used by Billy and his mates. There were a bunch of black kids looking after the boats by the side of the lagoon where we moored, and a few of the locals earned a scant living fetching and carrying for the white men, but apart from these, black faces were very scarce. Billy's beachside hangout was a pretty basic place – there were no proper bedrooms and only the most basic facilities. But for a couple of days of beach, beer and barbecues – which is what the expat workers come here for – it was fine.

Billy Graham was a traumatized man. When we turned up I got the distinct feeling that he had furnished himself with a little Dutch courage, but perhaps, in the circumstances, that was to be expected. I was going to ask him to recount an event that he would no doubt rather forget. If he had hit the bottle before our arrival, I couldn't entirely blame him. Eighteen months ago Billy had been kidnapped. His abductors had stuck him on a boat, taken him to a hiding place and held him for 26 days. He went without food for ten days, and during this time they forced him to dig his own grave and made him lie down in it. The pirates who took him were young – 'fresh out of secondary school,' he told me in his southern drawl – and he claimed to have known every one of them before the kidnapping.

Billy might have been traumatized by what had happened to him, but what struck me was that he was unwilling to blame his captors fully for what they had done. 'I was a victim of it,' he told me, 'and *they* were a victim of it. Nigeria is a place with great potential. Look around you.'

I did so. I saw sandy beaches and palm trees. The sun sparkled on the lapping water. Half close your eyes and you might be looking at a holiday brochure. 'It's fantastic,' I told him.

'Well,' Billy continued, '*we* get to live this way. The rest of the country does not.'

What Billy was telling me was the time-honoured tale of the haves and the have-nots. He believed that the terrifying experience he had undergone was a direct result of the differences between the rich foreigners in Nigeria and the indigenous poor. My next trip would take me to a place that threw these differences into even sharper relief. A place that I know I will not forget for as long as I live.

The residents of Ajegunle call it the Jungle. It's a bit of a misnomer. Jungles are green and fertile. Stuff grows there. You'd be hard pressed to find anything that grows in this desperate place.

Ajegunle is Lagos's biggest waterside slum. It's difficult to say how many people live there – like the rest of Lagos, the population is fluid and expanding. Estimates vary. Whatever the true figure, one thing's for sure – it's too many.

To get to Ajegunle from our hotel we had to drive through the perpetual Lagos traffic. Once we had freed ourselves from that snarling logjam, we drove through some suburbs that weren't, by Nigerian standards, too bad. I remember passing a school not far from our destination that wouldn't have looked out of place in a less impoverished part of the world, with big bright paintings of animals on the walls. But with a population so large, I knew it was only a privileged few that received the advantage of any kind of education. We stopped our car at the end of a long thin alleyway – perhaps half the length of a football pitch – and as we unloaded our vehicle we started attracting the usual attention. Locals approached us, intrigued by the camera gear and offering to carry it. In Africa, it's easy to assume that when this happens they mean to rob you, but that would be a lazy assumption. These people were poor, and like so many others they wanted chop-chop – a small tip for services rendered.

We walked down the alleyway. There was litter on the ground, but nothing out of the ordinary for Lagos. The further I walked, though, the more I could tell that there was something round the corner. Something unpleasant. A sudden stench filled the air – the sort of stench that makes you screw up your face, and which grew stronger and stronger the further we walked down that alleyway.

And then we saw it.

Ajegunle is hell on earth, its principal waterway like the River Styx. I half imagined the Devil cruising by in his speedboat, nodding proudly at a job well done. A couple of years previously, when I had travelled to Kenya to try and meet members of the Mongiki clan, I had visited Dandora, the biggest, most toxic rubbish tip in Africa. Ajegunle was like Dandora by the sea. The slum is so polluted that you can't see the riverbank for the rubbish that is piled up by the side of the water. To get to the main drag of the slum, we had to cross the river in one of the crowded punts that ferried the inhabitants back and forth. The water that carried us was thick with debris – plastic bottles, food wrappers, all manner of day-to-day waste that you or I would put in the bin, ready for the tip. But there are no bins in Ajegunle. It *is* the tip and this rubbish covers every spare space.

A large proportion of the population of the slum originates from the interior. In the Nigerian countryside most of what the people consume comes from the ground. It doesn't matter if they throw it away because it biodegrades. But in Ajegunle it's different. Like in most cities, food comes in plastic wrappers, in cartons and tins – stuff that won't biodegrade in a thousand years, that will stay precisely where you chuck it. While I was in the slums, I heard it said that the pollution was in large part down to the Western soft-drinks factory just a couple of miles up the road. Maybe that's true, but this wasn't just packaging. This was everything – the accumulated detritus of an overpopulated hellhole.

There were other kinds of waste here too. There is no proper drainage in Ajegunle, or sewers. The people who live in the Jungle defecate in the street. They don't clear it up because there's nowhere to put it, and because to clean up one turd out of millions would be a drop in the malodorous ocean. When it rains, what drains there are overflow and yet more raw sewage is coughed up onto the streets. As I wandered around Ajegunle that day I saw a sign advertising a 'Top Class Toilet', open to anyone willing to pay the few *kobo* it cost. These exclusive facilities, though, consisted simply of a toilet seat opening out onto the water below. You might get somewhere to park your behind, but you still have to shit into the river.

There are, strangely, a few semi-decent houses in this slum, raised above the water on stilts. They still look out on to the pollution, however, and in any case they are far outnumbered by run-down shanties cobbled together from sheets of corrugated iron, where families live, 12 to a room, in subhuman conditions. The electricity supply is erratic and unpredictable; open a window from one of these squalid dwellings and more than likely you look out into a gutter crammed with human waste and clouds of mosquitoes. And yet the people who live in Ajegunle are fiercely proud of their city. Some of Nigeria's biggest music stars come from here, and though it appeared hellish to me, the slum grows by the day. They're coming to Ajegunle in droves, and it's hard, from our comfortable Western perspective, to understand why.

It wasn't the first time my camera team and I had been the only white men in a slum, and you never quite get used to it. You do, however, learn certain techniques, and for me the only way of dealing with the inevitable attention is to plough on through the streets no matter what. As I set foot in Ajegunle, that's exactly what I did. It didn't stop me being a magnet for the inhabitants pushing their wares: it might have been early in the morning, but I hadn't gone more than 20 metres before I was offered palm wine by two men and sex by three girls. Could have been a very eventful morning, and it was an immediate reminder that street crime and prostitution were rife here.

We immediately attracted attention from other sources too. I'd barely set foot in Ajegunle before seven or eight big burly young men started following us and shouting, 'What you doing here? What you doing, *oyibo*? *Oyibo*, go! You have no right to be here! *You go!*' They were screaming, excitable and aggressive, crowding round us as we stepped through the rubbish-strewn slum. I barged through, away from our unwanted companions, but they managed to stop Will the cameraman and they weren't going to let him go any further, so we had to tell them what we were doing.

Our Nigerian fixer had arranged for us to meet a man who had been described to us as the chief of Ajegunle. He had lived in the slum for many years, and we had been told he had agreed to give us a tour of the area and explain to us some of the effects piracy had had on his community.

'We're going to see the chief,' I told them, naively thinking that this might buy our passage.

'What chief?' they shouted. 'Who chief?'

Will and I looked at each other with a bit of a sinking feeling. They seemed slightly less impressed than we thought they would be. What we didn't know was that, in true Nigerian style, there were about 15 different chiefs in Ajegunle, all self-appointed and all, as far as I could tell, vying with each other for whatever tenuous authority they had. Too many chiefs, you might say, and not enough Indians . . .

We told them the name of our man and they sucked their teeth, unimpressed. They stepped back, but it was obvious this was just a temporary reprieve for us. There was nothing else for the team and me to do other than press on into the slum – I had the distinct feeling that we wouldn't be allowed to turn back in any case – so we did exactly that. We couldn't shake our trail and before long we had a massive crowd following us, like a meteor with its long tail.

It was only 8.30 in the morning but already the sweat was pouring off me. We hadn't brought any water with us and I could feel myself dehydrating, but stopping for a leisurely drink was off the menu. It was clear as we went that nobody particularly wanted to be filmed. I had the impression that they were proud of where they lived and didn't want a white man to come there and look down on them. That wasn't what we were there to do of course, but I guess they weren't to know that. As our tail got bigger, however, it became increasingly clear what our new companions wanted. Chop-chop. They sniffed money.

We walked and we walked, the stench filling our noses, our shoes covered in shit. Eventually we came to the place where our fixer had told us we could meet our chief. It was hardly grand – a room on a platform on stilts overlooking the filthy water, the squalor and the degradation. There was a second room alongside it, also on stilts, and it was possible, if you were of a mind to risk falling into the filthy water, to jump between the two. By now we must have attracted a tail of between 150 and 200 people, all of them looking at us like we were a meal ticket. By that time all I wanted to do was get the hell out of Ajegunle. The mood was getting ugly. You could forget about interviews and pirates and TV shows – we had images of being mugged, or thrown into the shitty water, or worse. All we wanted to do was get away, but it was clear by now that the locals weren't going to let that happen. Not easily.

We crowded around the edge of one of the platforms. Inside the room all the local chiefs had congregated, along

127

with their advisers and their heavies. We were not invited inside as they argued among themselves, clearly working out exactly how much money they could rip us off for, and who should get what slice. On the other platform our followers thronged. You could see the stilts starting to sway and bend, and if too many people moved to one side, the whole platform would tilt precariously. Kids jumped from one platform to the other. I could envisage either one collapsing into the water at any moment, and I really didn't feel like a swim.

The chiefs carried on bickering. One of them was particularly lairy, and he looked like a cross between Oliver Hardy and Robert Mugabe. He was more despot than funny man, though, and he kept approaching us, telling us that *he* was the real boss and shouting that we didn't have permission to film here. He threatened to confiscate our equipment, and only backed down thanks to our fixer's attempts to smooth things over. Inside, the 'negotiations' continued, each of the chiefs saying their piece as we waited nervously outside, wishing that we were almost anywhere but there.

It was a riot of aggression and confusion, and to be honest none of us really knew what was going on. Eventually, though, they arrived at some sort of consensus and we were allowed access to *our* chief, an elderly man in traditional African garb, more quietly spoken than the others. It was clear, though, that the other chiefs were not fully satisfied with the outcome. I could tell that there was a good deal more aggro to come from them . . .

In the past, the people of Ajegunle had earned their living from fishing. The chief himself had fished the river for oysters and crayfish just 15 years ago. He took us out on a boat that chugged slowly through the polluted waters. Nothing could live here now, not in this soupy miasma of pollution. The chief echoed my very thoughts. 'There is no life in this water any more,' he said passionately. In order to find water clean enough for fish, you had to travel 20 miles out of Ajegunle. A big deal in a place whose main industry once relied on the health of the water.

As I had already learned, however, taking a boat out to sea off the Nigerian coast carried with it certain risks. The chief explained to me that many people were too scared to leave the filthy waterways of Ajegunle because of the piracy threat. 'They carry weapons,' the chief told me of the pirates. 'Sophisticated ones. They carry weapons that even our soldiers, our navy are not having in their possession.'

I wanted to know if the chief could shed any light on where these pirates were coming from. 'They migrate from anywhere,' he told me. 'Not from this community. They use masks to cover their faces. You cannot identify them.' He explained to me that if the pirates came across a fisherman, they would steal what little money he had on him. If there was no money, they would steal the fisherman's engine and net, then leave him to drift. 'Many are dying,' he told me. 'Many are wounded.'

Our chief spoke with real passion, and I didn't doubt that what he was saying was the truth. I wasn't entirely sure I believed his assertion, though, that none of the pirates came from Ajegunle. To rob a poor fisherman smacks of desperation, and I sensed that desperation was in plentiful supply in this slum.

I couldn't tell for sure if the pirates originated from places like Ajegunle or not, but I suspected that they did.

What was clear, however, was that they were having a devastating effect on an already devastated community. The people of Ajegunle were impoverished; their principal means of making a living had been taken from them on account of the astonishing levels of pollution; and now, if they tried to travel further afield to fish, they came up against the violent criminality of the pirates. It looked to me like a vicious circle, and there didn't seem to be any way out.

I couldn't wait to leave Ajegunle, but that wasn't possible. Not yet. We were still the focus of everyone's attention, and before we could get away from that godforsaken place we were told that we had to go and 'pay our respects' to the Oliver Hardy lookalike who claimed to be such an important man. Of course, we all understood what the phrase 'pay our respects' really meant. Ollie wanted chop-chop; otherwise we weren't getting out of there. It was about half past five when we arrived at his house, followed, of course, by the ever-present crowd of people. For such an important chief, it was a humble abode, although there was a whole row of people lined up outside – but Ollie was nowhere to be seen. It turned out that he was inside, having a kip – he'd hit the palm wine earlier that afternoon, got absolutely sozzled and was now sleeping it off.

When he finally made his appearance he certainly looked the worse for wear. He slurred his words, which didn't make it at all easy for us to understand him as his English was heavily accented anyway. As he demanded once more who we were and why we were here, he was a pretty comical figure. Under other circumstances we might have just laughed at him, or simply walked away, but that wasn't possible here. He might have been ridiculous, but we were surrounded by people who seemed to take him seriously. We weren't getting out of there until Ollie gave us the thumbs up, and for that to happen we needed to do some fast talking.

I stepped forward. The chief and his stooges fell quiet. And then, in a voice that made me sound like something between Captain Cook and General Custer, I spoke. 'We have come from far away,' I said.

Behind me, I could sense the guys suppressing their giggles.

'We have travelled many miles across Africa to search for pirates,' I improvised. 'To the Sudan.' (No, I don't know where that came from either – as the crew took great pleasure in pointing out to me later, Sudan is landlocked.) 'And now here.' I waffled on for a couple of minutes with my grandiose, over-the-top speech. And when I had finished there was a heavy silence.

I looked at the chief.

The chief looked at me.

And then he spoke.

'What?' he said. 'I am not understanding you.'

I blinked. And then, because he hadn't appeared to understand a word I'd said, I repeated the whole thing again.

My piece finished, the chief demanded to see the identity cards that we had been issued by the Nigerian government. He made a great show of scrutinizing these documents, looking us up and down as if we were obviously presenting him with forgeries, before revealing that he used to work as a passport control officer at the airport. So much for being the big chief of Ajegunle. Once he had satisfied himself that we were who we said we were, he started on a speech of his own. A long speech, telling us what an important man he was and how well he looked after his people. We listened politely, and were relieved when he finally finished. But then, to our dismay, one of his stooges took the floor. Another speech. More polite listening. Then a third. Then a fourth . . .

By this time we couldn't take any more. I stood up, announced that we'd really got the message, then nodded to our fixer. The time had come to cut to the chase. It was obvious that the only thing that was going to bring about our passage out of Ajegunle was hard cash, and so the fixer handed over a fistful of notes. It wasn't much in our terms – maybe about 50 quid – but I suppose to them it was a reasonable amount of chop-chop.

The deal was done. Our hosts' penchant for public speaking seemed suddenly to disappear. We took our leave, hit the streets and got the hell out of there. I'm no eco-warrior, but I've seen some dreadful things that man has done, and Ajegunle definitely makes the top ten.

9. The Juju Men

There are two kinds of piracy in Nigeria.

The first is purely criminal. It might be driven by the fact that the people are poor, but it is essentially armed robbery on water. The looting of boats in the quarantine zone of Lagos, the problems that prevented the fishermen of Ajegunle from casting their nets further afield: these were down to attacks from pirates who had a purely criminal motivation.

But there is another side to Nigerian piracy – a political side, carried out by insurgent groups in the Niger Delta. It is an irony that one of Nigeria's biggest problems is a direct result of one of its greatest assets. Oil.

I'd seen for myself in Ajegunle that while Nigeria might be oil rich, its people are some of the poorest in the world. But that only tells half the story. Standard Bank – one of Africa's largest financial institutions – estimates that over the past 37 years Nigeria has earned $1.19 trillion in oil revenue. That's 1.9 million million bucks. Nigeria's current yearly revenue from oil is around $40 billion. On the flip side of the coin, in the 30 years between 1970 and 2000 the number of Nigerians living on less than a dollar a day increased almost five-fold from 19 million to 90 million. The average income is less than that of Senegal, but Senegal doesn't export oil – it exports fish and nuts.

Forty billion dollars a year revenue; 90 million people on

less than a dollar a day. You don't need a PhD in advanced mathematics to work out that something's happening to the dosh.

Nigeria is one of the most corrupt countries in the world. According to the Economic and Financial Crimes Commission – Nigeria's anti-corruption agency – around 70 per cent of all oil revenue is stolen or wasted. It is thought that 85 per cent of all the money made from Nigeria's oil ends up in the pockets of 1 per cent of the population. Nigeria might be a place with huge natural resources, but it's also a place where the divide between very rich and impossibly poor is massive. A study in 2003 determined the top five most corrupt public institutions in Nigeria. The list goes like this: the police, political parties, national and state assemblies, local/municipal government, federal/state executive councils. It's a list that doesn't really leave much hope for the ordinary man or woman in the street.

The Niger Delta is the main oil-producing region of Nigeria. In 2008 it produced, on average, $2.2 billion of oil every month. The federal government is officially supposed to distribute about half of the country's oil wealth among the state governors, but because of the level of corruption, this money simply does not trickle down to the people. According to a report by Human Rights Watch in 2006, the government of Rivers State was awarded an annual budget of $1.3 billion. Out of this, the state apportioned: $65,000 a *day* for 'transportation fees' for the governor's office, $10 million for catering, entertainment, gifts and souvenirs, and $38 million for two helicopters. Health services in the same period received just $22 million.

As a result, the Niger Delta suffers terrible poverty even

by Nigerian standards. Less than a quarter of its inhabitants have access to clean water and very few villages have anything like what you and I would consider to be the most basic of amenities. The oil wealth that could have been spent on health and education for the millions of impoverished citizens of the Delta has been embezzled by the various layers of political corruption. Some of the money has even ended up in the UK. In 2007 a British court froze the assets of the former governor of Delta State, James Ibori. The frozen assets were said to amount to $35 million. While he was in office Ibori's official salary was $25,000. So either he'd been saving up for 1,400 years or he had other interests.

Extreme poverty is not the only consequence of the oil industry in the Niger Delta. It has also led to a shocking level of environmental pollution. Each year about 300 individual oil spills are reported, but the World Bank estimates that the true number could be ten times that. In 2008 reported oil spills amounted to 10,000 barrels, but individual spills can be bigger even that that – in 1998 one leak released 800,000 barrels. The effect this has on the environment is devastating. People living among the oilfields are constantly breathing in methane gas; a minor leak can destroy a year's worth of food for an entire community. Oil-infected waters have destroyed the fish population and have had a devastating effect on the mangrove forests of the Delta, with dreadful consequences for wildlife and humans alike.

The more I learned about the Niger Delta, the more I realized that while Nigeria's natural resources were highly profitable for a privileged few, and of course constantly propped up by our own oil addiction, the consequences of the oil industry were very bad news for the ordinary people of Nigeria. It was in the late 1980s that the dissatisfaction with their lot felt by so many of them turned itself into a series of insurgent groups.

The first of these groups to receive widespread attention was the Movement for the Survival of the Ogoni People (MOSOP). The Ogoni are a small indigenous group of around half a million, and their homeland – which they call Ogoniland – is located in the Niger Delta's Rivers State east of the capital city of Port Harcourt. They suffered more than most when the oil workers moved into their land. In 1990 MOSOP, led by the Nigerian environmental activist Ken Saro-Wiwa, started a non-violent campaign against the government and the oil producers. MOSOP drew up an Ogoni Bill of Rights which demanded a fair share of oil revenues and a reversal of the environmental damage that had already been caused.

In 1993 MOSOP organized peaceful marches by almost half of the Ogoni population, designed to bring the situation to the attention of the international community. Soon afterwards the Nigerian government embarked upon a military occupation of the area. The following year Ken Saro-Wiwa was arrested on bogus charges. He and eight other members of MOSOP were tried in what was widely agreed to be a kangaroo court. They were found guilty and sentenced to death by hanging. On 10 November 1995 the non-violent campaigner and his eight colleagues were executed.

MOSOP continued despite their leader's death, but the Niger Delta problem gave rise to several other groups, more militant than Ken Saro-Wiwa's organization. These included the Niger Delta People's Volunteer Force, led by Alhaji Dokubo-Asari. The NDPVF threatened 'all-out war' against the government. President Obasanjo offered Asari amnesty and money in return for the NDPVF's weapons, but soon reneged on the deal. Asari was arrested and remains in prison.

The latest, and largest, of these groups is MEND – the Movement for the Emancipation of the Niger Delta. They first came to widespread public attention in January 2006 when they kidnapped four foreign oil workers. Since then they have mounted sustained attacks on oil pipelines in the Delta, their stated aim being to reduce the country's oil production to the barest minimum. They have also continued their policy of pirating foreign ships and kidnapping foreign oil workers – 'white gold' as they're referred to in the Delta. In 2006 they kidnapped 80 foreigners. Between January and July 2007 they took more than 150. In 2007 the kidnap and ransom response company ASI Global rated Nigeria as being second only to Iraq in terms of kidnap threat; in the same year, foreign oil companies removed all non-essential personnel from the region.

MEND's job is made a good deal easier by the geography of the Delta – the network of mangrove swamps, creeks and channels that make it such a good place to hide. If you have a boat, you can move around the Delta virtually unseen; and of course you can take your hostages with you. It's pirate heaven. Or hell, depending on your point of view.

MEND's attacks on oil installations and their kidnapping campaign have had a direct result on the Niger Delta's oil output, reducing it by about a third. The organization has three main demands: the release of Alhaji Dokubo-Asari from prison, the receipt of 50 per cent of the oil revenue of the Niger Delta and the withdrawal of government troops from the region. Unlike Ken Saro-Wiwa's MOSOP, MEND positions itself decidedly at the violent end of the scale, warning the oil industry of its intentions in the following terms: 'It must be clear that the Nigerian government cannot protect your workers or assets. Leave our land while you can, or die in it . . . Our aim is to totally destroy the capacity of the Nigerian government to export oil.'

And they mean it. Their attacks have become increasingly bold. I was told by one trawler owner I met in Nigeria, who wanted to remain anonymous, that some vessels in the Bight of Benin fly special flags to indicate that they have paid MEND off in order to reduce their chance of being pirated. But the militant pirates don't only attack boats. In June 2008 MEND attack vessels hit the Bonga oil platform. This platform can extract up to 200,000 barrels of oil per day, but because it lies 75 miles from the coast it was generally believed to be out of the militants' range. That one attack shut down 10 per cent of Nigeria's oil production. The Nigerian government has attempted to downplay the organization's significance since MEND first appeared by saying that it's just a criminal gang and has tried to quash it by military force. To this end, they have established the Joint Task Force – a combined force taken from the navy, the army and the police – specifically to combat crime, militancy and piracy in the Niger Delta. The JTF was dispatched to the Delta under the moniker Operation Restore Hope – ironically the same phrase the United Nations used for their activities in Somalia that ended in the disastrous Battle of

Mogadishu. But if restoring hope truly is the aim of the JTF, it has quite a job on its hands: MEND know the area around the Delta much better than the government forces; they are better equipped and very well armed. (We heard rumours of a ship run by an enterprising arms dealer that sailed in and out of the region, a kind of floating gun supermarket. Whether this was true or not, I don't know, but there's certainly no shortage of weapons in that part of Africa.) And in any case, Nigeria being Nigeria, it is said that the JTF troops are far from squeaky clean. They have faced numerous allegations over the murder and rape of hundreds of civilians in areas thought to be militant strongholds – not exactly the best way of endearing yourself to the local population. The JTF is also unpopular in certain circles because in its struggle against MEND it is seen as protecting the interests of the oil multinationals and not the Nigerian people.

Conversely, the insurgents have the support of a large proportion of the public. Their aims are the aims of the common people: an end to poverty and government corruption. It is possible to buy on the beaches of the Niger Delta wooden models, about a foot long, depicting a boat with a couple of MEND militants – identifiable by a flash of red on their balaclavas – with two blindfolded *oyibos* in the back who have oil-company logos carved on their clothes. And people only sell these kidnapping mementos because there's a market for them among the locals. The Niger Delta, after all, is hardly a tourist hot spot.

It is of course the case, as happens with any such militant organization, that criminal gangs – in Nigeria they call them cults – have tried to get into the act, pirating and kidnapping for financial gain rather than political ends. MEND are savvy enough to distance themselves from such cults. In July 2007 they secured the release of a three-year-old British girl who was being held for ransom in Rivers State; in October 2008 they freed 18 oil workers who had been kidnapped for non-political reasons by people they referred to as 'sea pirates'.

In Lagos the pirates were purely criminal. From our point of view, this meant they had no reason to want to talk to us, no agenda that they wanted to promote. MEND, we thought, would be different. They had a drum to bang. They wanted their cause to gain attention. If we wanted to meet Nigerian pirates, they were our best bet; and if we wanted to contact MEND, we'd have to leave Lagos and travel south into the Delta. It wasn't a journey to be undertaken lightly, and the Nigerian authorities warned us against it. A delicate ceasefire between government forces and MEND had just collapsed, and the insurgents' policy of taking Europeans hostage meant that we would be very much in the firing line. Moreover, none of us had forgotten about Matthew Maguire and Robin Barry Hughes. They had been kidnapped by pirates five months previously and it was MEND who had claimed responsibility. The rumour was that they had specifically targeted British hostages because of a statement Gordon Brown had made in which he indicated his willingness to aid the Nigerian government should their ability to produce oil come under threat. All this meant that our plan to contact the MEND pirates was even more dangerous. But we knew that if we wanted fully to understand piracy in Nigeria, we needed to hear what MEND had to say. We needed to meet them.

So it was that we prepared to make the journey from Lagos to Port Harcourt, the capital of Rivers State, one of the nine states that make up the Niger Delta. We knew that MEND had Matthew Maguire and Robin Barry Hughes; we knew there was a possibility that they would see us as more desirable hostages. It wasn't too fanciful to believe that they would be willing to release Maguire for one of us. So it was that we forced ourselves to decide who, if push came to shove, should be the one to offer themselves up in that extreme scenario. In reality, the decision was already made for us. Everyone else in the crew had children. Everyone except the presenter. In retrospect it was a bit of a romantic notion, but I couldn't say I relished the idea of an enforced stay at the pleasure of the Movement for the Emancipation of the Niger Delta. Still, as we flew to the region that was their centre of operations, I couldn't shake the thought that it was a distinct possibility . . .

For the purposes of our investigations, we like to travel under the radar. Attract too much attention and people get nervous. Camera shy. They certainly start looking at you in a different way if they see you have security. I suppose that goes with the territory of searching out people who don't always want to be found. As we emerged from Port Harcourt International Airport, though, it was immediately clear that keeping a low profile was going to be a bit of an issue.

A team of armed police – uniformed and plain clothes, about 15 in all – was waiting for us; we were driven to our hotel by a police officer and our vehicle was flanked by police vans with wailing sirens. We cut through the thick, noisy, dirty traffic – people just got out of the way, and I would have done too – but it felt as if every man, woman and child knew we had arrived, and they stared at us as we passed through the busy streets. We couldn't have been more obvious if we'd tried. The security had been laid on at the insistence of the Port Harcourt authorities. From a safety point of view it made sense, I guess – every person with white skin in Port Harcourt is assumed to be an oil worker and is therefore a potential kidnapping victim. There are many such kidnappings a year from Port Harcourt and for us to be swiped would have been a high-profile calamity for the Nigerian authorities.

From an investigative point of view, however, it was a disaster. We were told that we couldn't go anywhere or film anything without our security team. They didn't leave us even when we arrived at our hotel. The lobby was crowded. We were later told that it was full of plain-clothes police, undercover government officials and MEND spies. Whether that's true or not I don't know, but I will say this: there were a lot of people hanging around in that lobby reading newspapers and doing not much else, and they didn't look to me like residents. I felt like I was living in a John le Carré novel. Before long, a creeping sense of paranoia started to ooze over us – a paranoia that would be with us for the rest of our stay in the Delta. I've been to some paranoid countries in my travels, places that make you feel uncomfortable for reasons you can't quite articulate. But the Niger Delta takes the cake.

MEND is a shadowy organization. Little is known about its power structure, and if its members want to hide they can easily do so in the Delta. We'd had an indication from people claiming to represent the movement before we arrived in Port Harcourt that they would be willing to meet us. But such people are by their very nature elusive. You don't just walk up to their doorstep and demand an interview. You don't summon them; they summon you. We knew we could be in for a long wait before that happened, so in the meantime we took to the street. I wanted to see the places these Nigerian pirates were known to frequent, and witness for myself some of the problems I had heard so much about.

Port Harcourt was different from Lagos. You feel even less safe walking round the town. The locals were noticeably more hostile towards white faces – you could see it in their aggressive stares. Our police escort didn't help matters because they were obviously even less trusted than the *oyibos*. This was hardly surprising: during my time in that town I saw members of the police force hitting people in the street for no apparent reason; I saw them bashing cars with their AKs. It wasn't exactly *Heartbeat*, and I have to say that when the coppers were out of sight (which didn't happen very often) I felt very, very white and very, very vulnerable. Never more so than when we were on the quayside. Bonny Island, the main terminal for all the crude oil extracted in the region, was just 40 minutes away up the creek. The waterways were filled with small elderly motorboats that ferried the locals up to Bonny Island and to the nearby villages. I didn't fancy taking my chances in one of those, not least because it was on this stretch of water that Matthew Maguire and Robin Barry Hughes had been pirated. I wondered how near or far away from us they were at that very moment, but in the Niger Delta it was impossible to know. Their location would only be known when – and if – MEND *wanted* it to be known.

Our fixer in Port Harcourt was a local independent journalist, a respected and intelligent man. He accompanied us everywhere and gave us the benefit of his knowledge. It was while I was talking to him, however, that I got one of my starkest ever insights into the difference between African culture and our own. We had driven, together with our always-present police escort, along a road that looked down into a nearby slum. This, our fixer told us, was where pirates and militants were known to live. From our vantage point on the high ground we could see that there was a shoot-out happening down below.

We turned to our police guard and asked them if I could go down to the slum and film what was going on. Predictably enough, I suppose, they shook their heads. 'No. You cannot go.'

I begged them. 'We really need to —'

Nothing doing. 'You cannot film this. You cannot go.'

I tried to talk them round. 'This is the whole reason for us being here. If we can't go and film this, what's the point?'

One of the policemen frowned at me. 'They have juju,' he said.

In West Africa, juju is a form of witchcraft. But it's not just something used to scare naughty children into good behaviour. Everyone believes in it. *Everyone.* The policemen told me that the pirates in the region had a special kind of juju that made bullets melt on contact with them. That was why they were so dangerous to approach.

I tried to keep my calm and turned to our fixer. He was a sophisticated man and I expected him to at least share my exasperation. But no. He was slowly nodding his head. 'It's true,' he told me. 'I have seen it. I have seen it with my own eyes.'

'Don't be silly, mate,' I told him. 'I've seen what a 7.62 round can do to someone and it doesn't melt on flesh and bone.'

But he was adamant. 'It does. I have *seen* it. And I will *not* go down there. You will not be able to shoot them and they will walk up to you and cut off your head with a machete.'

'I don't believe you. I want to go down there.'

'I am not going down there. *You* are not going down there. And you are not allowed to film.'

Sometimes you have to accept that you're flogging a dead horse, no matter how frustrating it might be. We weren't going down into the slum; we weren't going to get close to these gun-toting militants. And that was the end of that.

Our armed guards explained that the pirates achieved this magical effect by cutting their skin and putting some kind of leaf into their veins in order to make themselves like ghosts. And as we drove away from that shoot-out and a missed opportunity, I reflected that the fact that bullets patently did *not* melt on the skin of Nigerian pirates was actually immaterial. Our guards and our fixer believed it 100 per cent. They believed in juju in the same way a devout Christian believes in God. In a strange way that steadfast, unquestioning belief *made* it true in that the juju men reaped the benefit whether they were invulnerable to bullets or not. And it wasn't lost on any of us that if even an armed police unit was too scared to approach a shoot-out, the militants involved pretty well had carte blanche to do as they pleased. I might not have believed in juju, but it made the prospect of meeting with the juju men nerve-racking, to say the least . . .

10. A Drop in the Ocean

Our time in Port Harcourt was a frustrating one. We kept receiving emails and mobile phone calls from MEND, but at the last minute these meetings would always fall through. What we didn't know was that the militants were being heavily hit by the Joint Task Force at the time. They had other things on their minds than sitting in front of a camera for our benefit.

Constantly getting teed up and let down, though, had a bad effect on the camera crew and me. We know each other well, and we've been in dangerous places before – places where the bullets were flying – but nowhere compared to Port Harcourt for paranoia. If we *were* going to meet MEND, it would mean slipping out of our hotel room at night and trying to avoid our armed guards – an action that would probably get us arrested if we were caught. That in itself shrouded us in a sense of paranoid secrecy – the last thing any of us wanted to do was see the inside of one of the Nigerian jails, which by all accounts made Strangeways look like the Sheraton. But it was more than that. There aren't many places in the world where you're scared to leave your hotel compound, but Port Harcourt was one of them. Without wanting to sound in any way racist, in most places I'd travelled to I'd felt a vague sense of protection in being white. People might want to kill me, but the repercussions of them doing so would have been immense. You got the feeling that in Port Harcourt no one would give a shit.

Each night that we were on standby to sneak out and meet MEND, I would put calls through to two people in the UK, telling them that if I didn't call them again by a certain time they were to contact the Foreign Office immediately because it would probably mean we'd been kidnapped. Belt and braces stuff, but necessary under the circumstances. Still, not good for your frame of mind. As a result of all these strains, tensions between the crew increased. We started getting snappy with each other. It wasn't personal; it was simply something about that place.

We couldn't just stay in our hotel for days on end, though. While we waited for our meet to go ahead, we made a journey – along with our security guards / armed chaperones, of course – deeper into the Niger Delta, half because we wanted to see it for ourselves, half because we knew that this was the territory in which MEND operated and we thought our chances of catching up with them would be greater if we put ourselves where they were known to be. Ogoniland is a few hours' drive from Port Harcourt. Ken Saro-Wiwa's heartland, this was the region where oil was first tapped in the Niger Delta, and also the first region to rise up against the effects the oil industry was having on the people, their livelihoods and their environment. I was keen to see what it was like, but I could never have imagined the devastation I was about to discover.

Oil is no longer tapped in Ogoniland. The non-violent resistance of Ken Saro-Wiwa and MOSOP had the desired effect, forcing the oil multinationals to stop drilling in that region. There are still pipelines, though, and the infrastructure that goes with them. These pipelines are a target for the militants: only the day before, one of them had been blown up. The oil companies might have withdrawn from Ogoniland, but that didn't mean it wasn't still a dangerous place.

This is Africa as you'd imagine it. As our convoy drove along the mud tracks that led us deeper into Ogoniland, we passed thin men wearing ragged clothes, and nowhere did we see any signs of wealth. We stopped by a creek. There were fishing nets, wooden canoes and ramshackle huts. Progress had not come to Ogoniland, at least not to this part of it. You had the impression that the region looked much as it had done 100 years ago.

With one exception. A hundred years ago the area's natural resources had yet to be discovered, or exploited.

Our plan was to travel by boat up the creek and, unusually, our guards refused to come any further. The kidnap threat here was particularly high and I suppose they didn't want to risk it, their fully loaded AK-47s notwithstanding. Or maybe it was just because the boats all had holes in them and looked like they were about to sink. Up until now the presence of the guards had been a thorn in our side, but once we stepped into our wooden canoes and saw them and the shore ease away, we felt their absence keenly. We were about to enter the heart of the Niger Delta, and we knew that pirates, militants and kidnappers could be lying in wait around any corner, or hidden in the mangrove swamp. Not to put too fine a point on it, we were shitting ourselves.

Our guide as we slid through the water was a local man called Sonny. He sat in the back of my canoe, wearing a US Open baseball cap that looked decidedly out of place in this quiet, alien backwater. Sonny was taking us to see a damaged oil well head. It had leaked over a year ago and we were to witness the effect that leak had had.

It didn't take long for us to see what all the fuss was about.

As we paddled, I noticed a rainbow film on the oars, like the colours you see when a child blows a soap-sud bubble. This wasn't soap, however, and it wasn't child's play. Before long, you could see that the water was thick with globules of oil. You could smell it in the air too, the heavy, choking scent of crude. Here, miles from anywhere in the middle of the mangrove swamp, the air should have been clean and fresh, but instead it smelled like a petrol station. The further we went, the worse it got. If anyone had been so foolish as to light a match, God only knows what would have happened. We were warned not to use our mobile phones for fear that an electrical spark would ignite the fumes. About six months previously two guys had been killed in that way, and we were shown where the explosion had burned away a substantial part of the mangrove bushes. What a way to go. I was more than a bit worried about the wisdom of keeping the camera rolling because of the battery.

But roll we did, through the maze of dangerous swamps in the company of men we didn't know. Sonny explained to us that fish, winkles and mangrove crabs are important to the Ogoni people. It seemed they still managed to catch a small quantity of fish in these distressed waters, though it was astonishing to me that anything managed to live there. You might as well try and live in a petrol tank, and I certainly didn't see any sign of life as we continued our slow journey into the labyrinth. I didn't hear any either. It was deathly silent all around.

Sonny was a quietly spoken man who seemed friendly enough; we all knew, though, how quickly things could change. I couldn't suppress my nervousness as we continued to paddle through the polluted creek. It didn't take long for us to arrive at the well head. By now the creek was more oil than water, and our boats approached with care. It looked like an appalling piece of modern sculpture, a confusion of pipes and plumbing, surrounded by some sort of scaffolding. There would once have been a platform on top of this so that the black gold could be tapped, barrelled, put onto barges and exported. But now that the oil companies had withdrawn from Ogoniland, this was all that was left.

We circled the well head. Around us, we could see the mangrove bushes stained with oil – these are tidal waters, so when the water swells and lowers, it leaves its polluted trace on the surrounding vegetation. The fumes were chokingly thick now – they were in our throats and in our eyes – and the air itself was hot. Sonny explained that deep in the earth huge oil reserves were bursting to gush out. The only thing that was stopping that from happening was the small piece of machinery in front of us.

At least, it was *trying* to stop it from happening. Sonny pointed out the clunky network of plumbing at the top of the head. 'Can you see the oil coming up?' he asked me. 'If you look at that pipe up there, you can see something like smoke.'

I certainly could. A thick, cloudy vapour was hissing from the top of the well head – a bit like steam from a kettle, only this vapour was enormously explosive. There was also a constant, steady drip of viscous black liquid dropping into the water. The head might have been designed to keep the oil underground, but it clearly wasn't doing its job very well.

There were two possible reasons for the well head not functioning properly. The first was neglect. The oil multinationals had left the area; there was no profit to be made in maintaining what they had left behind and so it had been allowed to fall into disrepair. Not, as far as I could tell, an entirely unlikely scenario. But there was another possibility too: this head could have been one hub of an illegal trade that exists all over the world but which is prevalent in Nigeria. That trade is oil bunkering.

Bunkering is a fancy word for theft. It's big business in Nigeria – estimated to be worth $30 million a day. Looking at this leaking oil head, you could well understand why. It wouldn't be too much of a chore to bring a barge up to an outlet like this, attach a pipe to the plumbing at the top and simply tap off as much as you could carry. It appears that this is being done by all manner of people. Impoverished Lagosians can pump a little fuel into jerrycans; corrupt politicians and officials have the means to bunker oil on a rather grander scale; militants across the Niger Delta exchange bunkered oil for weapons. The bunkered oil is taken to offshore loading stations and then sold on into the world market. The International Maritime Organization estimates that about 80,000 barrels of oil were bunkered every day in 2008. Crime breeds crime, and Dr Sofiri Peterside, director of the Centre for Advanced Social Sciences in Port Harcourt, estimates that during 2008 a thousand people died in turf wars directly related to bunkering.

Sonny explained that bunkering could be done not only from a well head like this, but also from any one of the pipes that pump fuel across the region up towards Bonny

Island. All anyone needed to do was find a valve, open it and help themselves. Here on the water it was clearly more than possible that the oil dripping from this head was a result of illegal bunkering – someone had attached a pipe, taken what they wanted and failed to close up the plumbing properly.

It wasn't the sort of place you could stay for long. My eyes and throat were stinging from the fumes. The sky above was thundery and threatening. It looked like the heavens were about to open and I remember thinking that might not be a bad thing. Perhaps it would relieve us of the symptoms the oil vapour was causing.

We headed back down the creek and returned to the bank. By now any doubts we'd had about our escorts had dissipated a bit, but we were deeply shocked by what we had just seen. We loaded ourselves back into the car. Our tour of Ogoniland was not over yet – Sonny still had a few sights to show us. Although production had stopped here, there remained a huge network of pipes taking oil through Ogoniland to the terminals on the coast. Our convoy took us to the site of an old flow station and a new one. These places pump the oil offshore. We couldn't stay there long – this was an extremely dangerous place. The oil companies employ locals to protect the flow stations against oil bunkerers and militants. Ostensibly these people are employed to protect the community, but inevitably they divide it by overstepping the mark. It was just after we arrived when we received word that these locals already knew we were there and were on their way. Furthermore, they were armed. We knew that it was a very sensitive area to film, and that it was impossible to judge how our presence would be

On my way to another spill near Bodo, feeling slightly concerned about being kidnapped.

The angry villagers of Bodo speak out about the effect the presence of the oil companies has had on their livelihoods.

This villager believes that the only solution to the problem is to blow up the manifold.

God.

Governor Amaechi – or to give him his full title, the Right Honourable Rotimi Chibuike Amaechi, His Exellency the Executive Governor of Rivers State.

As requested we arrive at 7.30 in the morning, ready for our 8.00 meeting. But we were kept waiting . . .

. . . and waiting for two and a half hours . . .

. . . before finally being ushered in to see the man himself.

False alarm: we are asked to wait some more, and are offered breakfast – chilli doughnut with blancmange filling. There was also goat stew filled with bones.

The governor takes me on what is little more than a public relations tour of all the good works he has established in Port Harcourt.

He is a charming man, and genuinely popular with a lot of people, including these children we visited at a local school.

MEND – the Movement for the Emancipation of the Niger Delta. 'It must be clear that the Nigerian government cannot protect your workers or assets. Leave our land while you can, or die in it . . . Our aim is to totally destroy the capacity of the Nigerian government to export oil.'

Me in a MMEA (Malaysian Maritime Enforcement Agency) helicopter, patrolling the Malacca Straits for pirates.

From the helicopter I saw one of the nine radar stations positioned on small islands the length of the straits, which constantly scan the area for suspicious activity.

'Go go go!' Members of the MMEA board a ship and raid it for pirates as part of the training exercise.

Within minutes they have swept the ship, handcuffed the 'baddies' and have them all laid out on the deck, face down with their legs crossed.

Finally, red smoke is sent up to indicate that the ship has been secured.

The captain of the *Nepline Delima*, bearing scars inflicted by a pirate's machete.

Muhammad Hamid shows me a photo of the pirates lying face down after the boat was retaken.

Muhammad's bravery was big news in Malaysia; however, he cannot return to the sea and the job he loves.

I finally get to meet a pirate at his house in Batam. He asks to be addressed as 'Lightning Storm Across the Sea'.

With the pirates in a very small boat in the busy shipping lanes off the coast of Batam.

Storm and the other pirates explain the term 'shopping' to me.

A long walk in to 'Pirate Island', trying to avoid the highly poisonous stone fish.

Taking off the rough edges in order to make the bamboo less difficult to climb.

Being proved wrong! I witness five pirates in a tree.

Storm explains how the pirates slash the palms of any crew members who put up a fight.

We head back from the island in a torrential Indonesian rainstorm. There's no gold at the end of this pirate's rainbow.

Talking to a pirate's wife.
'He's a naughty boy!'

I meet with the pirates
for the last time.

Big business. I finally come face to face with a Somali pirate.

interpreted. Frankly, we didn't really feel like sticking around to find out. Time for a sharp exit, and on to our final destination for the day: another deserted well head, this time one which the oil companies claim to have cleaned up.

This head was on land but it looked very similar to the one we had visited in the creek. It too had oil fumes steaming, dragon-like, from its plumbing. The surrounding ground was one huge puddle of oil. 'So, as you see,' Sonny told us as we padded towards the well head, 'they have cleaned the spill. What they call "clean-up" has been done.'

It didn't look very clean to me. Oil was still leaking from the head and the surrounding space was dead and barren. Had it ever been cleaned up? Or had someone recently come along, bunkered oil and failed to seal the oil head properly? It was impossible to tell, but one thing was sure.

This place wasn't clean, and it wasn't healthy.

It was devastated.

Ledum Mitee is a lawyer and human rights campaigner in the Niger Delta, a friendly and intelligent man who received me in the yard of his Ogoniland compound. Following the death of Ken Saro-Wiwa, Mitee is the president of the Movement for the Survival of the Ogoni People. He had agreed to explain to me in more detail what it was that the inhabitants of the Niger Delta had to put up with. I asked him exactly what was threatening the survival of the Ogoni people.

'Oil was being exploited in front of people's houses,' he told me. 'In your backyard or anywhere. I grew up in a house that is about 200 metres from the nearest oil well. They spill occasionally. The only source of water that people have is stream water, and these rivers are themselves polluted. With gas flares 24 hours a day it makes it difficult for the crops to pollinate.'

The water they drank, the fish they fished for, the crops they grew – all these were being damaged by the oil industry. And I, as our fixer might have said, had seen it with my own eyes. But it wasn't just that. Ledum explained to me that the land was important to the Ogoni people not only because of what it could produce, but because of its spiritual connotations. 'It's where our ancestors live. You have the right to protect them, and if you don't, if the land is being desecrated, that portends some calamity to the community. Some forests that are sacred to the people are being felled for oil wells. We are not supposed to do that to them. The deities are annoyed.'

As Ledum spoke, I was reminded of the cultural differences that exist between the multinational oil corporations and the people whose land they are exploiting: the inhabitants of the Niger Delta were not only suffering environmentally and physically, they were suffering spiritually too.

MOSOP is a peaceful organization; Ledum Mitee is a peaceful man. I wondered what his thoughts were about MEND's less than peaceful modus operandi. He spoke frankly. 'The execution of Ken and the rest of my colleagues,' he told me, 'was intended to intimidate the rest. But it produced the opposite effect because most of those who have taken to militancy in other parts of the Delta cite our case as an example. They say, *you* were killed. *I* will not wait to be killed before we start killing.'

I asked him if he saw a direct connection between the piracy in the region, the militancy, the criminality and the pressure exerted by the JTF, the oil companies and the government. Ledum Mitee had no doubt. 'All these things are one single process. One reinforces the other.' The situation in the Niger Delta, then, was a vicious circle, and it sounded to me like it could only get worse.

I put it to Mitee that the environmental situation in Ogoniland was not just the fault of the oil companies – it was also down to the practice of oil bunkering. He agreed, and he enlightened me further on the gravity of the problem. 'There are three stages we found of bunkering. The first stage is those who cut the pipes and put it in jerrycans. Boys who are cutting the pipes in some areas and selling to the middlemen – those who have barges. And before you can be someone at that second stage, you must have a lot of connection and leverage, with armed, military people. Then you have those guys who will take it to the high seas where you have the big tankers. That is controlled by very, very important people who call the shots from Abuja. Last year, through bunkering, we lost almost $15 billion of oil.'

The bunkering of oil, it was becoming clear to me, was an illegal act on the water – yet another form of piracy, and the sort of sums Mitee was talking about were staggering. The government's own anti-corruption task force estimates that $400 billion has gone missing since oil was first discovered in the Delta. And as with so much of the corruption in Nigeria, it occurs at the highest level. You don't get the oil out into the open market without the help of people in authority. That means the government. Once it enters the world's fuel supply, there's nothing anyone can do about it – chances are that you or I have filled up our cars on illegal bunkered oil without even knowing it. You can see the attraction, both for the corrupt politicians in Abuja and for the poor of Ogoniland – if you've got gold right on your front door, chances are you're going to grab a handful.

I'd been shocked by what I had seen in Ogoniland. But as we'd been driving around our guides had told us that there was a village called Bodo on the outskirts of the area that was even worse. So the next morning we decided to take a look. In order to get to this new oil spill we needed to head further up the river. The canoes we had been in the previous day would be no good to cover that kind of distance, and so we boarded a small fleet of lifeboats with outboard motors. I say *we* boarded – in fact we were piggybacked onto the boats by our guides, who insisted that we shouldn't risk wading through that polluted river.

We sped through the confusing network of waterways. The plan was to stop off to see the oil leak, then move on into the village of Bodo itself. So it was that we moored at the edge of the mangrove swamp, alighted from our boats and set off in search of oil.

The spill that they took me to was on a much more massive scale than those I had seen the previous day. All around, the mangrove – which takes hundreds of years to grow – had been killed. The ground itself was a soggy, muddy, oily mess; you could touch it with your fingers and they would come up stained black. The closer we drew to the source of the leak, the blacker the earth became. I felt like I was sinking in a quicksand of black gold. The mud itself was hot because of the oil – so hot that it started to cook my feet. Eventually we just couldn't walk any further.

These pipes have been there for many years and they don't have an indefinite lifespan. Sooner or later, they're going to split. Bunkering is doubtless a big environmental problem in the Niger Delta, but it's not the only one: the area suffers from an ageing oil infrastructure that hasn't been maintained and is causing devastation such as that which I was looking at now. The underground pipe had obviously been leaking for a long time, and eventually the oil had spurted to the surface. It's very difficult to find the source of such a leak and it takes a long time – time during which the environmental damage accumulates. This leak had been fixed a year ago, but it was clear that its impact would last for tens, maybe hundreds of years to come. It was hell on earth, and I was shocked to learn that oil spills such as this happen, on average, once a day in Nigeria.

The boggy ground around the oil spill wasn't the sort of place you wanted to stay for long, so we returned to our boats and headed up towards Bodo. There we disembarked again. As we entered the village we received the familiar hostile looks – the fact that we had white skin naturally made the locals think that we were oil workers. Not their favourite people. When it became clear who we were, however, they grew a little less antagonistic, even eager to talk to us and explain what was happening to their home.

The villagers were angry with the oil companies and the effect their presence has had on their lives. A crowd of them gathered round me, and their spokesman spoke vehemently about the lack of compensation they had received. 'We are fed up,' he said. 'This is our river. This is our only source of livelihood. Over 80 per cent of this community depends on this river. Look at all the people – you can see that they are all hungry. If this river was OK the way it was, all these boys would be on the river struggling for their daily bread.'

I looked towards the river. The boys he was indicating weren't working – they were larking about in the filthy, oily water.

'But because they have nothing to do,' the villager continued, 'every day we fight with them that they should not commit stealing and all that.'

The story I was hearing was similar to the one I had been told in Ajegunle: because of the pollution, people were turning to crime in order to put food in their bellies.

The villager continued. 'All this militancy is attributed to it. Their pipes should be removed from our land. Our source of livelihood is destroyed now. And one of these days they will hear from us, because the solution would be to blow up the manifold. And we will. We *will*. I am saying to you we will. We are going to blow down this manifold and let the government come and kill all of us. So let them kill us with their guns instead of we die of hunger.'

Truly desperate words. It would have been easy to mistake them for mere rhetoric, but the crowd of villagers hanging round their spokesman showed no sign that they disagreed with him, and he spoke with a real passion. Part of our reason for travelling into the Delta was to try and make contact with MEND. We hadn't done that, but we had certainly learned why they exist and why they have support among certain sectors of the community. The villagers in Bodo honestly believed that the pollution was killing them. It was causing crime and misery. Under circumstances like that, it's perhaps understandable that people might want to take things into their own hands, and that their measures are likely to be extreme . . .

Bodo was an edgy place. It smelled like a refinery, and we were covered in oil. The kids offered to clean our boots for a few dollars – cheap for the kind of work they had to put in, but I still have those boots and they still reek of oil.

The day wasn't over yet. As we sped back, I was in a boat with our journalist fixer and four or five of the locals who were showing us around. Suddenly, for no apparent reason, our boat peeled off down a tributary, away from where the others were heading.

And in the Niger Delta, that's not a good thing to happen.

I felt my stomach turn to lead. *Oh fuck*, I thought to myself. *This is it. We're being taken.*

Nervous people on planes are known to look at the faces of the air stewardesses if they hit bad turbulence. If the cabin crew look nervous, they know they should panic. Similarly, I quickly glanced at our fixer, hoping to see a reassuring expression of calm. Not a bit of it. He looked as alarmed as I felt – with a sinking feeling of a lift you can't get out of that is hurtling to the ground.

'Where are you going?' our fixer shouted. 'WHERE ARE YOU GOING?'

Our guides looked blandly at us. 'Short cut,' they said.

'No,' the fixer said. '*No! No short cut.*'

By now the others were well out of sight. We were entirely under these people's control: we couldn't have escaped even if we'd tried. The only way out of that boat was into the water, and you'd have just drowned in the oil. I muttered nervously, doing my best to at least *look* calm. 'Can we just turn round?'

They looked at us like we were mad. Truth of the matter was that our boys were racing the others. But not in my head they weren't. In my head we were about to spend a few months enjoying the hospitality of the Niger Delta pirates.

There was a moment of stand-off. Our guides insisted that they wanted to take their short cut; I found myself nervously reflecting on an uncomfortable fact I had heard. Apparently, a substantial proportion of people, male and female, who are kidnapped in West Africa get raped. And – close your eyes now if you're of a squeamish disposition – not always with a penis. Bits of wood, bits of metal . . . It's a way of dominating someone. There was a good deal of buttock clenching going on. Not that that would have helped.

Eventually, our guides relented. We turned back, caught up with the others and made it to shore safely, but we'd had a quick insight into how easy it would be to kidnap someone in that network of channels. I don't think I fully relaxed until we were back in our armed convoy heading out of Ogoniland and back to Port Harcourt.

We were only in that part of the Delta for a short time, during which it was difficult to get a real handle on the ins and outs of the environmental damage that was being done there. The oil companies claim that the leakages are solely down to the mismanagement of the well heads by the many people illegally bunkering oil. It appeared to me that this was true in some places, but not everywhere, and you'd be hard pushed entirely to absolve the multinationals of blame. Whatever the truth, one thing was clear to me. The oil bunkerers were doing very nicely out of what was going on in Ogoniland; the oil companies weren't doing too badly either. The losers were ordinary citizens and the environment. Having seen this at first hand, even if I didn't agree with their methods, I could well understand why militant political groups like MEND existed.

In June 2009, a few months after I left Nigeria, one of the multinational corporations, Shell, made a payout of $15.5 million to the families of the Ogoni Nine, including Ken Saro-Wiwa's son, in settlement of a legal action in which it was accused of having collaborated in their execution. Shell did not concede or admit to any of the accusations, but by avoiding a lengthy court case they stopped the world at large becoming more aware of the environmental situation in the Niger Delta. A large proportion of that money will be used to pay the Ogoni Nine's legal costs, but a sum of $5 million has been put aside to set up a trust for educational and community projects in the Niger Delta. The trust's name is Kisi, which means 'progress'. And maybe it is progress of a kind. I can't help thinking, though, that in a country that produces $40 billion of black gold a year, $5 million is just a drop of oil in the ocean.

11. Kidnap Alley

Back in our Port Harcourt hotel, we returned to our prisoner-like existence. Subject to the whims of the MEND spokes-men, who would occasionally get in contact by phone and then let us down, we couldn't go anywhere without our armed guards, who were there for our protection but also to make sure we didn't go walkabout. We wanted to be low-profile, to melt into the background, but that was proving impossible. To make our predicament worse, we then received an official invitation to visit the governor of Rivers State early the next morning. We were bleary-eyed because we'd been up half the night waiting for phone calls from pirates. But we were also in Port Harcourt as the governor's guests and couldn't do anything without his permission. So in a way it wasn't so much an invitation as a summons.

Governor Amaechi – or to give him his full title, the Right Honourable Rotimi Chibuike Amaechi, His Exellency the Executive Governor of Rivers State – is taking a hard line on piracy. He's one of MEND's biggest adversaries, and a bit of a maverick within the Nigerian political system. The government had recently passed a law giving all kidnappers an automatic life sentence, but Amaechi himself had supported increasing that to a death sentence. The word was that he had plans to turn Rivers State from the most volatile area in the Niger Delta into a thriving megacity, with skyscrapers and a monorail. If that was the case, he certainly had his work cut out. He had a hard act to follow too. One of his predecessors, Peter Odili, faced accusations over the theft and mismanagement of billions of dollars' worth of oil revenue. However, he has since been granted immunity by a government anti-corruption investigation. I guess that's just the way it works.

Even if I resented being escorted to his offices with the kind of close protection I'd never previously had, part of me was curious to see what this optimistic hardliner was like. As we headed through Port Harcourt, we saw evidence of Amaechi cracking down on other illegal acts too. All too frequently we would pass houses – many newly built – with red marks on the door. These marks indicated that the houses had been built without planning permission, and the governor's zero-tolerance administration had ordered that they were to be knocked down. So even before we arrived I had the impression that Amaechi meant what he said.

We arrived at the governor's office, as requested, at 7.30 in the morning, ready for an 8.00 meeting, and were asked to go through the sort of security cordon you'd expect at any airport. But if Amaechi was keen to see us, as he claimed to be, he didn't have a very good way of showing it. We were kept waiting in the lobby for two and a half hours before finally being ushered in to see the man himself. It was a bit like getting in to see the pope, what with all the goons and stooges and layers of security. Amaechi was obviously a popular man, but he was only the governor of one state of one region of Nigeria. It was immediately obvious, though, that maintaining his administration required a *lot* of money – you could tell that not only from the layers of bureaucracy and security that surrounded the man, but also from the relative affluence of the building. Amaechi looked younger than I expected – all the photos and paintings of him I'd seen around the place had been retouched to make him look older and more imposing.

Amaechi wasn't quite ready to talk to us, so he offered us breakfast while we were waiting. He led us into the breakfast room, an ornate space with a large table surrounded by gaudy but not inexpensive chairs. Breakfast consisted of typical Nigerian cuisine. I wasn't a big fan of the chilli doughnut with blancmange filling; there was also goat stew filled with bones – as in many places I've been, the animal had clearly been carved with a hammer. I certainly wouldn't want to slag off the way the Nigerians eat – it's their cuisine, and they adore it. No doubt they find the idea of bacon and eggs a bit odd, but what was to their taste wasn't hugely to mine, and I'd have done anything for a bowl of cornflakes.

After hours of waiting, the moment finally arrived for us to have a bit of face time with the governor. He was a charming man, in his way. You could see how he might be a popular politician, and he smiled politely at me as I asked if I might talk to him about some of the issues he had inherited when he took over.

I asked the governor what his take on MEND was. His face became a little less smiley. 'I don't think there is anything called MEND,' he replied. 'I have not seen one.'

Really? So there was no Movement for the Emancipation of the Niger Delta?

'I've not seen one. Let one person come forward and negotiate with us. I've not seen one. I can't say whether they exist, but I've never seen one person called MEND. So far

164

the people I have been dealing with in the Rivers State have been criminals.'

So was it the governor's viewpoint that the people calling themselves MEND were using their organization as a political excuse for criminal actions?

'Yes. Ninety-nine per cent of those involved in Rivers State are criminals. Simple.'

I asked him about his support for the death penalty for acts of piracy and kidnapping. He explained to me that in Nigeria robbery attracts the death penalty. Kidnapping, from his point of view, was even worse – the robbery of a person. He believed that his calls for the death penalty were popular with the people. 'You should go to the streets,' he told me. 'The people are tired of these criminals. So it's quite popular. It may be unpopular with the NGOs, civil rights or human rights movements, but it's popular with our population.'

Amaechi had told me I should hit the streets of Port Harcourt. I wondered if he would accompany me. Ever-obliging, he agreed. 'Let's go,' he said.

The governor then took me on what was little more than a public relations tour of all the good works he had initiated in Port Harcourt. It was a curious excursion. He insisted on driving me himself, to show what a man of the people he was – it helped though that he had an armed convoy around him, with a Russian DshK heavy machine gun mounted on a pickup and 20 men with assault rifles clearing the path of traffic ahead of us. To give the guy his due, however, he didn't appear to be afraid of getting his hands dirty. As we were travelling down the highway we saw a local trying to extort 'taxes' from another driver; the driver was

refusing and the extortionist had attacked him. When Amaechi saw this, he ground to a halt, jumped out and ran across
the highway. 'What are you doing?' he demanded forcefully,
before turning to his guards. 'Arrest that man!' he instructed.
A bit later on we were in one of Port Harcourt's incessant
traffic jams when we spotted a white army van going the
wrong way up the road. Again, he stopped the car, jumped
out and made the van turn around and travel the right way
up the road, those inside apologizing to everyone as they
passed.

As we toured the town righting wrongs like some kind
of West African Judge Dredd, I asked Amaechi about the
piracy that blighted the region. What were the reasons for
it, in his view, and what could be done to stem the problem?
I was half-expecting more of the hard-line dogma, but in
fact he showed himself to be sensitive to the causes of
Nigerian piracy. 'Poverty,' he told me. 'Most of those people
who are involved in crime now used to go fishing. Now
there is nowhere to fish. The military government that we
had lacked the courage to enforce discipline and government control, which is what we are doing now.' But the
piracy was a direct result of poverty. After all, he said, 'Who
would want to carry guns and rob people at sea if they can
feed themselves?' You don't take the kind of risk involved
in committing acts of piracy, he maintained, unless you
know you have a risk of dying of poverty.

We were given a tour around a new hospital Amaechi was
building, power plants, schools and other worthy projects. I
couldn't help noticing, though, that there were a lot of half-
finished construction sites. When we stopped to look at one
of these, Amaechi approached the Italian contractor, who

happened to be on site. 'Why is this not finished?' he demanded. 'What is wrong? *Why* is it not finished?'

The contractor looked, I thought, a bit nervous. 'Do you want the real answer?' he asked. 'On camera?'

'Of course,' Amaechi stated. 'You can be honest.'

'You haven't paid me.'

That smooth smile spread over Amaechi's face once more. 'We will pay you, my friend,' he said. 'You do not need to worry about that!'

But the contractor looked worried, and I had the distinct impression that his worry derived from the fact that telling the governor of Rivers State that he was downing tools might have consequences for more than his bank balance. Maybe he just felt the same sense of paranoia that we all did in this town. I don't know.

I wasn't so naive not to realize that our excursion with Governor Amaechi was little more than a PR stunt, but even so it struck me as he walked around the town that he was genuinely popular with a lot of people. I was left to consider that I had seen a number of different sides to the same story. The political piracy, kidnapping and industrial sabotage carried out by MEND was clearly a big problem for the area. As with many militant groups who seek their ends by unacceptable means, their grievances were real. I'd met ordinary folk who sympathized with MEND because their lives, frankly, had been ruined by the awful consequences of bunkering and oil spillages. And now I'd met the administration, whose principal aim was to crush the militants and the criminality with which they were associated, and that administration had its supporters too.

The only people I hadn't managed to connect with were MEND themselves. And truth to tell, I was beginning to wonder if we ever would.

That night MEND once again told us to stand by, to wait for another call that would tell us where to go, and when. Yet again we prepared to slip away from our security under cover of night; yet again the call never came. The trouble was this: the Joint Task Force had been carrying out a sustained attack on MEND bases in the area. Either the militants thought it was too dangerous to meet us at that moment in time, or they just weren't in a position to do it. And so the following morning – exhausted and a bit demoralized – we took the decision to cut our losses in Rivers State and travel elsewhere in the Delta. If we could get closer to some MEND strongholds where the JTF *hadn't* been active, maybe we would have more luck.

The town of Warri is 95 miles from Port Harcourt in neighbouring Delta State. The security goons who had been tasked with accompanying us seemed very anxious that we should leave early, and we soon found out why that was. To get there, you need to travel up a road which has been dubbed Kidnap Alley. No prizes for guessing why. The journey from Port Harcourt to Warri takes about six hours; if we left too late, the security boys would have to come back down Kidnap Alley in the dark. Not to put too fine a point on it, they were shitting themselves at the prospect. These were burly, armed policemen – a fair indication of how dangerous the road was. While we were en route, we would occasionally have to stop by the side of the road to take a leak. Whenever that happened, the guards' paranoia increased a hundred-fold. They really didn't want to be there.

The journey was made slower by the fact that we were forever being stopped at checkpoints by local police looking for chop-chop. We managed to stream some Eddie Izzard from an iPod to the car radio – surreal stuff at the best of times, but doubly so when you're driving up Kidnap Alley. This didn't please our driver. He wanted to listen to his tribal beats – fine for 20 minutes, but six hours of it would send you east of Barking. I'd never seen our guards look so happy as when they dropped us off at our hotel in Warri. Not even a goodbye – they were instantly gone in the hope that they could get back to Port Harcourt before it was dark.

Now that we were out of the jurisdiction of Governor Amaechi we no longer had to contend with the ever-present personal security. That didn't mean, however, that we were entirely free agents. There was a heavy police presence around our hotel, and we were told in no uncertain terms that we would be stupid to leave. Travel into town, they said, and you'll get killed or kidnapped. The hotel, though, was not the sort of place where you really wanted to spend any time. When we arrived, I was greeted by the hotel owner. 'We have a big room for you, Mr Kemp,' he said, and led me proudly up.

It was a big room all right, but that was all that could be said for it. At some stage the door had been pulled off its hinges, then inexpertly replaced using screws without proper threads. I'd been given one of those plastic key cards, but there was no point because you could just open the door without it. Not that you'd want to. Inside, parts of the walls were spattered brown and red. It was either ketchup and brown sauce, or it was blood and shit. The carpet was mysteriously sticky. The shower curtain stank of mildew and there was a bucket by the toilet so that you could flush it, as the cistern didn't fill properly. There were mosquitoes everywhere and it was obvious that the bedclothes hadn't been changed in a long time – they were black with grease from other people's bodies, and there was a dent in the pillow from when it had been last used. The sort of bed that makes you itch just looking at it.

But this was our hotel and we had to make do. We once more started to put out the feelers, to make calls to contacts that we had. And then we did the only thing we *could* do. We waited.

And waited.

Confined to our hotel for our own safety, we just had to hope that the nearby MEND bases had escaped government attacks. But there was no way of knowing, and our lines of communication were worryingly silent. We waited for several days and nights, long past the time when we should have been on a plane out of there. There's only so long you can wait in a hotel room in 40-degree heat, with shit on the walls, having read the same book four times. As each day passed, it became increasingly clear that MEND were unlikely to get in touch – we could only assume that they'd been hit by the JTF – and we were going to have to bail out. It was increasingly clear that the programme we wanted to make wasn't going to happen. With the frustration of failure weighing heavy on us, we finally decided there was nothing more we could do. We would have to return to Lagos empty-handed.

Once the decision was made, we moved quickly. We

wanted to be on the next flight out of there. We packed our gear up like madmen, knowing we had to shift sharpish if we weren't going to miss our plane, and we asked our fixer to organize a couple of cars to the provincial airport nearby. Somehow he forgot, which only made our rush through the go-slows of Warri even worse, but we finally got to the airport. Strangely we were recognized – a white oil worker even came up and asked me to sign a *Gangs* book for them – but all our attention was focused on splitting. Warri, we had decided, was far too much of a worry. The queue at the airport seemed to last for ever. When the time came for me to put my hand luggage through the scanner (it was the day pack I used in Afghanistan) I saw it slip into the machine before the conveyor belt stopped. One of the security men addressed me.

'Who is your big boss?' he demanded.

By now I'd lost all patience with Nigerian bureaucracy. 'We're an autonomous organization,' I told him facetiously. 'We don't have a big boss.'

'What?' He had suddenly been joined by a number of others. 'We need to speak to your big boss.'

'We don't have one.'

'We have to know. We need chop-chop.'

I shook my head. 'There isn't any chop-chop. Can I have my bag back, please?'

'No. We need chop-chop.'

I shook my head again, then put my hand towards the machine to drag out my bag.

'If you put your hand in there,' a female security guard snapped at me, 'we chop it off.'

I froze. She half looked as if she meant it.

'We need chop-chop,' she insisted.

But by now I'd truly had enough. I raised my voice. 'I'M NOT PAYING CHOP-CHOP.' Everyone in the terminal must have heard me. They all looked towards me and sucked their teeth at the *oyibo* kicking up a fuss.

I looked back along the queue. Ewen, our director, was only a few positions down. 'Look,' I said. 'You want chop-chop? Ask him.' It was a bit of a three-billy-goats-gruff tactic – I felt pretty sure that Ewen in his six-foot-four Glaswegian way would make it very clear that they weren't getting any chop-chop from him either. I went through and stood back to watch the fireworks. Funnily enough, the Nigerians came off second best in that little argument. I think they'd just picked the wrong batch of exhausted, disillusioned, pissed-off foreigners to tap for cash.

We returned to Lagos, and then to London, feeling that we had failed, but maybe we were being too hard on ourselves. It was true that we hadn't managed to meet MEND or any pirates. But in our time in the Niger Delta we had certainly gained an insight into why the pirates do what they do. I couldn't condone what was happening in the Niger Delta – kidnapping, murder, acts of terrorism – but I felt that at least I could now understand why it was happening. The political piracy in the Delta and out at sea – like the criminal piracy in the quarantine zone of Lagos or the petty piracy that hits the fishermen of Ajegunle – had its origins in abject poverty and the environmental degradation that was ironically a direct offshoot of the fact that Nigeria was so oil rich. And perhaps it's fair to say that the biggest pirates in Nigeria are the people in power, those who, as Ledum Mitee had explained, made millions from selling bunkered oil on the open market.

As I think back on my time in Nigeria, I wonder if I was too harsh on it. Maybe I just saw the wrong side of the happiest country in the world. But I can't help thinking that with all that potential wealth, it should be a lot happier than it is. That annoyed me, and saddened me.

When we left, Robin Barry Hughes and Matthew Maguire were still being held somewhere in the Niger Delta. On 20 April 2009 Robin Barry Hughes was released for health reasons; Matthew Maguire was set free on 12 June 2009, having been held hostage for nine months. When we admitted we'd been in the Delta trying to find him, he told us we were mad. He probably wasn't far wrong. It wasn't long after our departure that government forces escalated attacks against militants in the Delta and a blanket ban was placed on all journalists in the area. Had we waited a couple of months, we couldn't have gone there even if we'd wanted to. And as I write this book MEND have just destroyed another pipeline in the Delta. The problems of that region are far from over.

Our global search for piracy, though, was to take us elsewhere, to the most famous pirate-infested stretch of water on the planet: the South China Sea. We had already learned that searching for pirates could take us to the most unexpected places, and none of us knew what we would find when we got there . . .

PART 3
The South China Sea

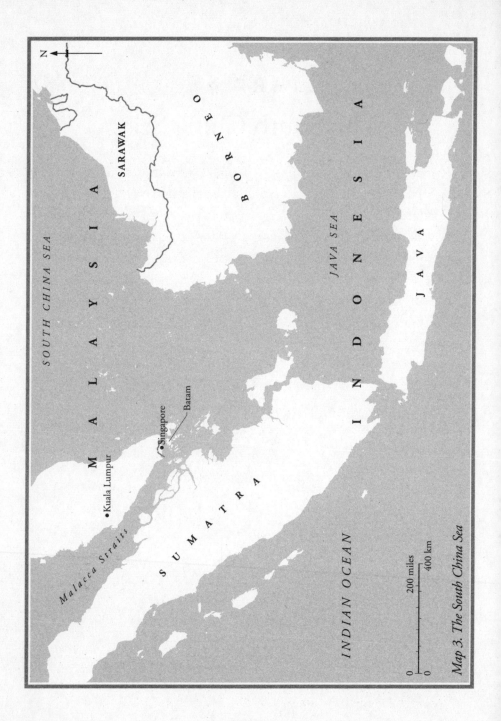

N

SOUTH CHINA SEA

BORNEO

SARAWAK

MALAYSIA

JAVA SEA

INDONESIA

JAVA

•Kuala Lumpur

•Singapore

Batam

Malacca Straits

SUMATRA

INDIAN OCEAN

0   200 miles

0   400 km

Map 3. The South China Sea

12. The Malacca Straits

In 2005 the merchant vessel *Nepline Delima* was making its way north up the Malacca Straits, a narrow stretch of water bordered by Indonesia on the west and Malaysia on the east. It was night-time when it came under attack by a ten-man group of pirates armed with machetes and machine guns.

The *Nepline Delima* was an oil tanker, carrying $12 million of oil, and a classic example of a low-freeboard vessel. Valuable and vulnerable. In this instance, however, things didn't go quite according to plan for the pirates. Their attack was thwarted by a young member of the crew. His name was Muhammad Hamid, he was just 27 years old, and his story is one of great bravery. His actions that night could certainly have got him killed, and for all he knows that may happen yet. He agreed to meet us in his small village somewhere on the Malaysian mainland, but only on the proviso that we did not reveal where this was. This young man was living, along with his family, in fear.

Muhammad explained to me what happened the night the pirates came to call. 'The captain made an announcement: "Help! Help! There are pirates on the boat! Get up, boys! Get up!" They broke into the captain's room and attacked him with a machete. The crew ran away.' As he spoke he showed me pictures of the captain, his slashed face patched up and bandaged.

The pirates chased the crew all around the boat; moments

later Muhammad could hear his friends being beaten. 'So I hid,' he told me simply. He secreted himself under the bed in his cabin. At one point the pirates, who were searching for him, entered his room and the light from their torches illuminated his knees and chest, but by some miracle they didn't see him. Knowing that the pirates must have arrived by boat, he then snuck away from his hiding place, looked over the edge of the ship and located their vessel. He climbed down the outside of the ship into their speedboat. 'When I got into the boat, I was able to cut the rope. Finally I was free. I was safe.'

Muhammad might have been safe, but his crew mates weren't. He knew he had to do something, but he had never driven a speedboat like this before. It took him ten minutes to fumble around in the darkness for the ignition button before he was able to get the boat moving. Even then, he had only the vaguest sense of where he was and, more crucially, which direction he was supposed to travel in. But luck was on his side. He travelled 50 miles, through rain-storms and high seas, to shore. He stopped a couple of times for a cigarette to calm his nerves, and who can blame him? After five hours he ran out of fuel, but managed to locate a spare canister that the pirates had stashed away.

While Muhammad was trying to find help, the crew of the *Nepline Delima* were all put into one room, where they were, quite literally, pissing themselves. They all assumed that their shipmate was dead.

Muhammad finally hit land. Immediately he alerted the powers that be and told them that there was a pirate attack occurring right now on his ship. But the authorities didn't believe him: for whatever reason, they thought at first that

Muhammad was a pirate himself. Eventually, though, they accepted his word and an operation was mounted to retake the *Nepline Delima*.

Muhammad explained to me what happened. 'The police promised them that if they surrendered, they would let them go free.' The pirates bought it, but of course the police had no intention of keeping their word. There was a six-hour stand-off, at the end of which the crew were released and the pirates arrested.

A happy ending, but there was more to this story than met the eye. It later transpired that the first officer and another member of the crew were in league with the pirates. They had delivered the coordinates of the ship for a piece of the pie. The first officer was later released, but the rest of the pirates were sentenced to seven years in a Malaysian jail. As for Muhammad Hamid, his life will never be the same. His bravery made a big splash in Malaysia, but he now feels unable to return to the job that he loves. 'If I sail again, they might just find me,' he said. He feared that the families or associates of the pirates would take revenge on him. Kill him. Hence his new life of enforced anonymity.

Muhammad was a brave man, and a lucky one. If the pirates had caught him trying to escape, chances are that he'd now be dead.

The Straits of Malacca are the second-busiest shipping lane in the world, after, believe it or not, the English Channel. Flanked by Malaysia and Singapore on the east and Indonesia on the west, it has historically been, and remains, an important channel for vessels making the profitable journey from China to India. It is also the most direct route from the bustling ports of south-east Asia to the Persian Gulf and up through the Suez Canal to Europe. Put simply, it's full of boats, and those boats are full of goods.

And this has been the case for centuries. In the days before oil became the world's most valuable commodity, spices were transported in vast quantities through the Malacca Straits and they were worth a great deal to the Europeans of the eighteenth and nineteenth centuries. Much of the European colonization of south-east Asia was driven by the desire to control the spice trade, and as the quantity of high-value shipping increased in these waters so, inevitably, did the incidence of piracy.

Pirates had roamed the Straits of Malacca long before that, however. Just as the corsairs and buccaneers had been used for political reasons as private additions to countries' naval might during the Golden Age of Piracy, so in the fourteenth century a local ruler by the name of Parameswara was able to fend off his land-hungry neighbouring rulers by keeping the pirate crews of the Malacca Straits onside. If you were to travel to the bottom of these waters, the skeletons of old ships and the watery graves of generations of sailors would be a testament to the historically turbulent nature of the South China Sea, a stretch of water that has always been feared by seamen.

The Malacca Straits and the South China Sea are no less turbulent now. In 2008 there was, on average, one pirate attack a week here. Singapore itself has the second-busiest port in the world. Each day 1,000 ships travel through its sea lanes, carrying a quarter of the world's maritime trade and a third of its oil needs. Such a high quantity of shipping, of course, presents an easy target for pirates and until recently pirate attacks were so bad that the Malacca Straits were designated a war zone by Lloyds of London, with insurance premiums to match. The truth is that if you're the owner of a merchant vessel and you choose to send your ship through the Malacca Straits instead of via a longer, and therefore more expensive, route, you're taking a gamble.

From a personal point of view, south-east Asia has a certain family resonance. My Uncle Tom was married to my nan's sister Olive. During the Second World War, as a captain in the British army, he was stationed on the island of Singapore. This was a crucial strategic location, the site of the main British military base in south-east Asia. It fell to the Japanese on 15 February 1942, in part due to a surprising tactic by the enemy. Rather than attack the island, as had been expected, by sea, they sent their troops overland across Malaysia on bicycles. What followed was a rout. The Allies were forced to surrender and Winston Churchill called it the 'worst disaster' and the 'largest capitulation' in British history. Around 80,000 Allied troops became POWs, and Uncle Tom was one of them.

I know only too well that there aren't many pleasant ways to spend a war. But if there were, several years as a Japanese POW wouldn't be one of them. Uncle Tom was set to work on the Burma Railway. Designed to link Thailand and Burma, the line was important to the Japanese precisely because without it they had to bring supplies and troops to Burma through the Malacca Straits, where they were a target for Allied submarines. Its construction came at a high price. The film *The Bridge on the River Kwai* is based around the Burma Railway, but the events of that movie are largely fictitious. The truth would be too gruelling to watch. The line became known as the Death Railway: an estimated 16,000 prisoners of war died constructing it, but that figure is dwarfed by the 90,000 Asian workers who perished.

Uncle Tom never talked to me about his time as a POW, but I subsequently heard stories. If a group of prisoners failed to lay their allotted length of track on any particular day, they'd be woken up the next morning at an irregular time. Their guards would then force them to dig a grave. When it was done, they would, at random, shoot one of the POWs dead and leave his mates to fill in the hole. After the Japanese surrender, the POWs were so emaciated that the British government did not want the public to see them in that state. Uncle Tom was sent to Canada to recover, and so he didn't see Olive until a year after he was rescued. For someone who had undergone such terrors, Uncle Tom was a lovely man. Sensitive. During his time as a POW he used to write poetry on the back of the few cardboard Red Cross boxes that got through, using blood or flower stamens as ink. But I have a childhood memory of seeing the skin on his stomach, marked and scarred from where he had been beaten with split bamboo sticks.

So it was that, as a child, this part of the world held a horrific mystery for me and I felt strange about making my first journey there. My first port of call, however, would not be Singapore but Kuala Lumpur, the capital of Malaysia. It very much feels like a city plonked in the middle of the jungle. All the time I was there I had the weird sensation that the jungle was only just being kept at bay, that given half a chance its tendrils would wrap themselves around the buildings and reclaim the land taken by the city. It was hot, cloudy and humid when I was there, with intermittent rain. And when it rained, it rained – some of the biggest thunderstorms I'd ever seen. You wouldn't want to be at sea in some of those. I liked the Malaysian people: my impression of them was that they were tough, hard-working and intelligent. Their capital city came across as a place that was thriving.

Kuala Lumpur is home to the Malaysian Maritime Enforcement Agency. The MMEA had been in existence for about four years. Its main role is to combat piracy and it has been surprisingly successful against massive odds. It comprises members of the Malaysian armed forces, and they had offered us the chance to meet one of their admirals, then join them on their patrols and training exercises.

We met the admiral on a boat patrolling the straits. He explained to me that their jurisdiction covered the eastern, Malaysian, side of the straits, which comprises about 640,000 square miles of water. Not as big as the Gulf of Aden, but still a sizeable stretch and one which includes 1,400 miles of coastline. Every month, he told me, 70,000 vessels pass through it. One of the most dangerous areas for piracy, he explained, is the southern mouth of the channel, near Singapore. This was for two reasons. First, because the channel gets narrower here, ships have to slow down to avoid collisions. And second, any vessel heading into the port of Singapore has to wait its turn. It wasn't as bad as the quarantine anchorage in Lagos, but it did mean sitting still for a while. And as I'd already learned, if a ship's sitting still, it's much easier to hit.

When it came to piracy in the Malacca Straits, the admiral knew his onions. 'There are three types of activity normally,' he told me. The first was straightforward petty theft. Opportunism. The pirates board a ship, steal whatever they can get their hands on and then disappear. The sort of thing that was happening in Lagos on a daily basis. A second, less common, pirating technique was a variation on the kidnapping theme. The pirates would commandeer the ship, then nab the captain or some of the crew and disappear with them. The ship itself would be allowed to sail free, but the hostages would be held to ransom.

The third type of piracy the admiral described to me was rather more elaborate. The pirates commandeer the ship and let the crew go. They then repaint the whole vessel, change its name and use it for their own ends. 'It becomes,' the admiral told me, 'what we call a phantom ship.' This might sound like an unwieldy operation, but there's plenty of ocean in which to hide these vessels, and it seems to be the case that they are sometimes pirated to order. Chosen like food off a menu. Indeed, according to the admiral, some of the piracy in the Malacca Straits is highly organized. Pirates have people within the harbours who have access to all sorts of crucial information – the nature of the ships' cargos, where they're going and where and when they have to slow down – so they can choose the best place to intercept them.

Sometimes shipowners fail to report piracy attacks to the authorities. This is because they don't want their insurance premiums to increase – a bit like you or I not claiming when we bump our car to avoid losing our no-claims bonus. But I had also learned from other sources that there are unscrupulous owners who are more than happy to get into bed with the pirates and take the insurance companies for a ride. In such a case, the shipowner might let the pirates know where and when to hijack his ship. He will take the insurance money, and let the pirates sell the vessel, at which point he also takes a cut of the sale. Everyone's a winner – except the insurance companies, and of course the traumatized crew . . .

The admiral also told me that he believed certain shipowners were willing to pay pirate organizations a fee to ensure their safe passage. I was reminded of the trawler owner who admitted that he paid MEND in order to sail safely round the coast of Nigeria – from what the admiral was saying, this was a fairly common practice.

The MMEA don't just patrol the Malacca Straits by ship; they also use helicopters, looking out for suspicious vessels from the air. They have their work cut out. I'd learned in Nigeria that, as a pirate, you're at a huge advantage if you have an easy waterside hideout. In the Niger Delta the massive complex of waterways provided just that. Here, the geography wasn't much different. As I joined an MMEA helicopter and we rose high above the water, I immediately got a fix on the maze of mangrove swamps that line the coast. It was a marbled landscape of thin waterways and green trees. You could hide a boat in there and never be found, no matter how many helicopters were swarming above you. The admiral had explained to me that pirates in these waters always make sure they operate relatively close to the coastline. That way, if they are observed, they can quickly get into the mangroves before the authorities have the opportunity to catch up with them. The MMEA were looking into new imaging technologies to help them see pirates in the dark and when they're under cover, but even I could tell that the most sophisticated thermal imagery would be no good in these mangrove swamps. There would be all sorts of life hidden in that foliage. Only some of it would be pirates . . .

As we flew over a fishing village called Crab Island, I asked the MMEA officers who were escorting us what sort of boats the pirates favoured. What, exactly, were the officers looking for?

'Normally they use a fast boat, a small boat that is more manoeuvrable than a ship, because you need to catch up with a big ship in order to close in and do your activity.'

Down below, I noticed such a boat and asked if we could follow it. We did so. The owners were clearly just fishing, but from that height I could see how easy it would be for them to slip into the mangrove and immediately out of sight.

'So, Ross,' the pilot said. 'You tell me. How are you going to prevent them from coming in and out? There's so many places where they can hide.'

It was impossible, I agreed. Even if you had another hundred helicopters.

The channel between Malaysia and Indonesia is particularly narrow – about ten miles at its tightest point – and this makes it even tougher to police because pirates can slip from the Indonesian coast to the Malaysian side with ease. And if I thought the Gulf of Aden was busy, I was about to have my eyes opened. The Malacca Straits were non-stop. It was obvious how pirates would be attracted to this area like bees to flowers. From the helicopter I saw one of the nine radar stations positioned on small islands the length of the straits, which constantly scan the area looking for suspicious activity. But despite this surveillance, and the military presence of the MMEA in the skies above, ships are still advised to travel through these waters at high speed in order to make them that bit less susceptible to piracy. I saw one such vessel moving at above the magic figure of 12 knots. The ship itself had a fairly low freeboard and four enormous cranes on its deck. These cranes meant that it could load and unload itself without being reliant on the infrastructure of whatever port at which it might dock. That in itself made it a very valuable piece of equipment, regardless of what sort of cargo it was carrying. If you were a pirate and came across one of these vessels, you'd see dollar signs. No wonder it was shifting.

If a ship does get pirated in these waters, the Malaysian government has the facility to react in the form of the MMEA's own elite force, who are specially trained to retake ships. I was invited to go along with this special unit on a training exercise to see just how sharp they were, and what they were capable of. These guys were well armed, carrying Heckler & Koch MP7 submachine guns, and in their black gear and balaclavas they looked impressive.

It may only have been a training exercise, but it was enough to give me an insight into just what a dangerous job these guys have. We congregated on an operations ship in the middle of the straits. This ship had been supplied to the Malaysian government by the Japanese. The Malacca Straits are particularly important to Japan. It's politically too sensitive for them to send their own navy into these waters, however, so instead they supply the Malaysians with equipment such as this. A kind of insurance premium to ensure that their shipping doesn't get hit. The Japanese, after all, for all their wealth and success, are an island race, utterly reliant on shipping for their prosperity. If Japan's shipping lines were cut off or seriously compromised, the country would soon crumble. Eighty per cent of its oil comes through these waters, and Japan lives or dies by its trade.

From the Japanese boat, along with this heavily armed task force, the camera crew and I boarded a couple of RIBs, which sped – and I mean *sped* – towards a target vessel, a tugboat which had been hijacked by 'pirates' holding the crew. As the tug came into view, I couldn't help thinking that if this were a real-life operation, if the pirates we were apprehending were real-life pirates, I'd be feeling pretty damn vulnerable. It's true that by the time this special forces unit is on its way, with a sniper in the helicopter hovering overhead for air support, the game would be up. Any right-thinking pirate would put his hands up and do the time. But there are always a few loose cannons, and if the pirates did decide to put up a fight and open fire on the SF unit, there's no doubt who'd be more vulnerable – and it wouldn't be the boys in the tug. A few GPMG rounds into the hull of that RIB and it would sink, and you'd have a pretty good chance of killing everyone on board. The sea offered the commandos no protection, and they were dangerously exposed.

We travelled at motorbike speed, covering the half-mile or so to the tug immensely quickly, our bow wave spraying into our eyes. The two RIBs took up positions on either side of the tug and the commandos boarded with a lot more speed and expertise than I did. Instantly they were swarming over the tug, shouting at each other in the international language of special forces: 'Go go go!' Within minutes they had swept the ship, handcuffed everyone and had them all laid out on the deck, face down with their legs crossed so that they could easily see if anyone was preparing to stand up. Uncross your legs and you're a threat: in a real-life situation, that would mean the commandos might get to use those MP7s. One of the crew pointed out which of the captives were pirates – as far as the guys were concerned, everyone was a potential threat until proved otherwise. Finally, red smoke was sent up to indicate that the ship had been secured.

It was a slick operation. It might only have been an exercise, but it was a crucial one for the unit if they were to keep their skills honed. This particular unit had already been called upon to intervene in genuine piracy situations 15 times, and they knew that number 16 could happen at any moment.

We returned to the Japanese ship and headed back to port, sharing snakefruit – an indigenous fruit so named because of its scaly skin – with the MMEA maritime police. As we were entering the harbour, they clocked a boat coming in from Indonesia, which they pulled over. It was a fairly big boat, about half the length of a football pitch, and shaped a bit like a junk. The unit searched the vessel and it became clear that it was totally brimful of contraband. There wasn't a single bit of unused space. All sorts of things that you or I wouldn't think of smuggling were on board: chickens, pigs, ducks and, most valuable of all, Viagra, or a version of it – a growth industry, I'm told. (There's a massive business in fake pharmaceuticals in this part of the world, and while a few fake Viagra tablets might just render someone a bit floppy, there's a much more serious side to this racket. Imagine someone with HIV taking what they think are antiretroviral drugs to keep themselves alive, when in fact it's just salt and water . . .) Smuggling between Indonesia and Malaysia is commonplace – the maritime police could have stopped any one of the ships making that short journey and had a good chance of finding someone up to no good. The crew seemed pretty matter-of-fact about being nicked; the contraband was confiscated and the skipper knew he could face a penalty of some description. I don't know what that would be, but even he looked rather as if it was all in a day's work.

13. Lightning Storm Across the Sea

The job of policing the Malacca Straits is difficult, but the actions taken by the MMEA and the Malaysian government have had an effect. Some people think that Lloyds declaring it a war zone was the catalyst that made the Malaysian authorities wake up and smell the coffee; others that they would have had to do something about it at some stage. Whatever the truth, while it is undoubtedly the case that piracy remains a problem, it has decreased in certain parts of the straits as a result of the authorities' efforts.

When I had spoken to Muhammad Hamid, however, the brave young man who had thwarted the pirate attack on the *Nepline Delima*, he had given me an interesting nugget of information. The pirates who had taken his ship came from a place called Batam, a small Indonesian island (one of the 17,500 that make up that disparate country) situated just 12 miles off the coast of Singapore. This coincided with other information we had been given. The MMEA admiral had indicated that many of the pirates had moved their field of operations further to the south-east. It struck me when he said this that the MMEA's operations had not so much *stopped* piracy, but forced the pirates to work somewhere else. There's a lot of sea out there, and there's no way you can police it all.

It made sense that Batam, positioned right at the mouth of the Malacca Straits, would be a pirate hangout. So if I wanted to get close to Indonesian pirates, that small island sounded like the place to go. On the map it looks like just a quick hop, but with 20-odd bags and all the administration that goes with taking camera equipment from one country to another, it's not like that. Flying to Singapore from Malaysia is, of course, entering a different country, as was the boat journey from Singapore to Batam. Malaysia to Singapore to Indonesia is not a straightforward trip, especially for a camera crew.

Batam is the same size as Singapore – about 275 square miles. But that's where the similarities end. Singapore is rich and bustling, thriving from its position as a major international hub and financial centre. Batam, separated from Singapore by just a few miles of water, couldn't be more different. It's a poor place, with about a fifth of the population of Singapore. Those people that have jobs work in traditional industries such as fishing and manufacturing, but the gulf between the haves of Singapore and the have-nots of Batam couldn't be more stark. The shores were lined with rickety wooden dwellings supported on stilts; across the water you could see the gleaming skyscrapers of Singapore. The poverty here wasn't as bad as that which I'd seen in, say, Ajegunle, or maybe it was just the case that there was less desperation here. In Ajegunle rubbish lined the streets; here you had the impression that people might be poor, but they were more aware of their own environment. Parts of the island have even tried to establish themselves as tourist destinations. Away from the shanties there are a few beach resorts, and of course you get a great deal more for your money than you would if you were holidaying on Singapore island.

Still, poverty is poverty. Batam might have a small holiday industry, but it also has the problems that often accompany economic deprivation. It is, for example, a well-known destination for sex tourists, especially popular with the rich of Singapore in search of a dirty weekend. There are also known to be at least ten groups of pirates operating off the island. Batam is dominated by the shipping lanes. Look out to sea and you can't help but be impressed by the massive number of enormous merchant vessels that fill the skyline. I could well believe that if you were of a piratical frame of mind, the sight of all that wealth might be too much to resist, especially if you didn't have the means of making a living any other way. Or even, to be honest, if you did . . .

My hope was that by heading to Batam we could finally come face to face with modern-day pirates. Once again we knew that our best chance of achieving our ends was by staying inconspicuous; once again we looked like being thwarted. When we arrived at our hotel there was an electronic display in the foyer with rolling news and stock market prices. I was bleary-eyed and jet-lagged, but my eyes soon opened when I saw something flash across the screen. 'Welcome to celebrity ROSS KEMP!'

I blinked, then turned to the guys. 'Did I just see that?'

'See what?'

'My name, up on that screen.'

They shook their heads. 'Don't be stupid.'

I agreed with them, perfectly willing to believe that with the jet lag and exhaustion I'd been seeing things. But then I looked up again.

'Welcome to international celebrity ROSS KEMP! Staying here for five nights only!'

I turned to the guys again. 'You saw it this time, right?'

They nodded their heads slowly. 'Yeah, we saw it.' So much for our top-secret undercover investigation.

We'd been tipped off that the pirate gangs hang around the many pool bars that line the docks, waiting for their next job. So it was that on our first night in Batam we headed down to one of these bars with a couple of local fixers. They were grubby, low-rent places, the sort of joints where you could well imagine people of a criminal tendency hanging out. Smoky. Dimly lit. While we took up residence in one of the bars, our fixers moved to a neighbouring establishment, asking questions and gently probing the locals, trying to get an in with a Batam pirate who might be willing to speak to us while we did our best to keep a low profile.

That first night, though, there was nothing doing. It was with a vague sense of déjà vu that we headed back to our hotel room empty-handed, desperately hoping that we weren't about to relive our frustrations in the Niger Delta.

That evening in the pool halls, however, paid off. As a result of our under-the-counter enquiries, one of the pirate commanders of Batam agreed to meet us. It was a turning point in our investigation. We had travelled all over the world in search of pirates. We'd witnessed acts of piracy at first hand, and we'd experienced some of the factors that led desperate people to become pirates. However, although we'd come close – agonizingly close – to meeting actual pirates, we'd always fallen at the final post. Now was our chance, and I was a little apprehensive as we drove through the busy streets of the island, dodging the traffic as we made our way, finally, to meet a pirate.

The principal mode of transport on Batam, as it is all over south-east Asia, is the 50cc motorcyle. You see them everywhere and soon get used to their constant wasp-like humming. I've seen six people on one of these things – Dad driving and the rest of the family clinging on wherever they can like a hugger-mugger version of the Royal Signals Motorcycle Display Team. There are no people carriers for the poor of Batam. The vehicle that we were follow-ing, the one that was supposed to be leading us to our pirate, was not a motorcycle but a small silver car. The irony wasn't lost on me. To find a pirate, I wasn't going to sea but following a car, weaving among the overloaded motorbikes. But as I was beginning to learn, trouble on the water is directly linked to trouble on land. In a weird kind of way, it made sense.

As we followed the vehicle – and attracted glances from the locals, for whom Europeans were clearly a curiosity – I couldn't help but feel a bit dubious that this was anything other than a wild goose chase. We'd been let down too many times before to get our hopes up.

This time, though, our local fixers were on the money.

When we were a mile from the pirate's house, we stopped filming. The conditions of our interview were, reasonably enough, that we revealed neither his identity nor his location – not that I would ever have been able to find my way back there. But, in accordance with his request, we refrained from turning on the camera again until we were inside his house. A nice house, with a four-by-four parked outside. Clean. Well kept. It was a far cry from the poor buildings and shan-ties you find elsewhere on the island. If the balaclava'd man sitting in front of me genuinely was a pirate, as he claimed to be, it struck me that his line of work was definitely keeping the wolf from the door. What surprised me was that this had the hallmarks of being a religious household. A piece from the Bible was displayed on one of the walls, but in the background you could hear regular calls to prayer from two nearby mosques, reminding us that Indonesia is a Muslim, not a Christian, country.

In order to keep his identity secret, our pirate insisted that we use a fake name. 'What do you want me to call you?' I asked.

He spoke an indecipherable phrase, and our translator giggled. I turned to her. 'What does he want to be called?'

'He is called Lightning Storm Across the Sea.'

Modest, huh? It sounded like a bit of a mouthful to me. 'Do you think it would be all right if we just called him Storm?' I suggested.

She nodded. 'Yes, I think so.' And so it was that I found myself sitting down with a balaclava'd pirate called Storm. Over the years I flatter myself that I've become something of an aficionado in balaclava wear for the discerning criminal. To be honest, though, I wasn't quite sure what Storm was wearing. Maybe there's not much call for such items in Indonesia, but Storm's headwear had a distinctly home-made look. I couldn't help wondering if in one of his drawers there was a jumper with an arm missing.

I didn't dislike Storm. There was a calmness about him. Perhaps that's something that comes with being at sea for a long time. I don't know, but I could tell that he wasn't shouty or showy. As I grew to know him better, I learned that although he treated us with respect, he had a ruthless side. Calculating. Mess with him while he was going about his business and you'd surely regret it. He was the leader of a small group of pirates, some of whom I would meet later. That didn't mean, though, that he was entirely autonomous. Storm admitted to me that he took orders from someone further up the line to target certain ships, and I wanted to know who that person was.

Nothing doing. 'We don't know who the boss is,' Storm told me. 'This is Mafia law.'

Either Storm genuinely didn't know, or he wasn't going to tell me his name, and I could understand why that might be the case. He wasn't referring necessarily to the Italian Mafia, but it was clear that he was a cog in the wheel of some bigger crime organization. I doubted that his bosses would have taken too kindly to their names being revealed just because Storm wanted to get on the telly.

Storm wouldn't reveal the names of his masters, but he did shed some light on how his instructions, and the information about which boat to take, filtered down to him.

'Sometimes the crew gives us information. They give us the coordinates, the location of the ship that must be attacked.'

Knowing what I knew about the *Nepline Delima*, Storm's words rang true; the MMEA admiral had also hinted at this. Inside jobs – *Treasure Island* for the twenty-first century.

Storm went on to explain what happened to a ship once he and his colleagues had taken it. 'Up to the buyer,' he said. 'If it's wanted in Europe – no problem. If it's wanted in Asia – no problem. Sometimes it can take two weeks or even a month.' Quite an operation – these guys were substantially more than hit-and-run merchants, and there was clearly a lot of money involved in what they were doing.

Storm explained that most of the time when a ship is hijacked in this way, a buyer is already lined up – they don't just do these jobs on spec. But occasionally 'they want the boat to be lost because they need the insurance money to buy another boat'.

Once the pirates had delivered their boat to its designated destination, they would catch a flight back to Indonesia as part of the deal. So far, so sneaky. But a pirated ship has a crew, even if some of them are in cahoots with the hijackers – they would be lightly beaten up for the sake of appearances. But what happens to them then? Storm spoke matter-of-factly. 'We tie them up, blindfold them and leave them on an island,' he said. 'Or we put them on a raft and send them away.'

It was sounding more and more like *Treasure Island* by the minute, and I was struck by the fact that some things, at least, hadn't changed all that much since the Golden Age of Piracy, when pirated crews would be left on an island as a matter of course. Nowadays it's easier to locate somebody abandoned in this way, but crews can still potentially be marooned for quite some time. I wondered what they did for food. Or did the pirates just leave them to starve?

'They're human too,' Storm replied. 'They must be fed and not left to die.' That, at least, was something.

It was clear that in Storm's line of work you needed to be armed. I wanted to know what sort of weapons he and his buddies carried. 'Machete,' he told me. 'But I don't always use it.' You can bet your bottom dollar, though, that he *threatens* to use it, and when I put that to him Storm just nodded.

My Indonesian pirate had spoken in an honest and straightforward manner about what he did and how he did it. He might have been hiding his face behind his balaclava, but I didn't have the impression that he was hiding the truth. On the contrary, he appeared, if anything, proud of his activities. He saw himself as a professional, and demanded the respect that came with it. And as a proud professional, I wondered what he thought about his more high-profile Somali cousins, the ones who had so successfully eluded us in the Gulf of Aden. Storm was rather dismissive of them.

'In Somalia they board the boat and start shooting,' he said as if that was an act of the highest foolishness. 'You don't do a job like that. The pirate from Somalia is a stupid pirate. They're not in our class. They're low class in Somalia.' Pirate envy? Storm definitely thought that he and his boys were a cut above the rest.

Storm and his comrades didn't just make their living from big hijacks and insurance jobs. Like in any business, they knew that downtime was time when they weren't earning, and so they filled up the quiet periods with an activity known as 'shopping'. Storm explained to me exactly what this was. 'That's the term used by the pirates in Batam when we board any passing ship, just take the money and go.'

Hijacking they do with the cooperation of the crew; shopping is another matter. The piratical equivalent of smash and grab, it's a lot less risky than hijacking a ship, and the rewards are potentially great – especially as you can hit more than one ship in a night. I asked him if the crews generally put up any resistance when Storm and his gang went shopping. 'Some will fight back,' he said quietly, 'but we are not afraid of them. If they want to fight, we will kill them.'

199

He sounded almost prosaic as he said it. Cold. There was something scary about that lack of emotion, about the fact that he wasn't trying to be the big man but was just saying it as it was.

I didn't doubt that he was telling the truth.

For whatever reason, Storm and I seemed to get along. He offered to take us out into the busy shipping lanes off the coast of Batam so that he could show me exactly how they operated and which ships made good targets. In order to do this, we linked up with another guy who wanted to give himself some sort of Dick Dastardly name – I think it was Ghost of the High Seas. More inventive than 'Mr Smith', I guess, but we tried not to show that we found their monikers amusing.

Going out to sea with a troop of balaclava'd pirates has its risks. Storm and Ghost were clearly dangerous men but I didn't feel, for the moment at least, that they were likely to give us any problems. And it wouldn't have been difficult to pick Ghost out of a line-up, even with a balaclava, because he had wingnuts which made him look like he was wearing ear defenders. The authorities, though, were a different matter. The waters of Batam were highly patrolled – if we were caught in the company of pirates, we would have a lot of explaining to do. To keep our profile lower, Storm suggested we rent a traditional fishing boat – long and low and with a small outboard motor. To be honest, the vessel wasn't really fit for the job. It wasn't much more than 15 metres in length and a couple of metres wide. Into that space we had to fit me, two pirates, someone steering, a translator and three camera crew. A boat like this simply isn't designed to come up against the wakes of the kind of shipping we were likely to encounter, and being heavily weighed down with bodies didn't help matters. We were a mismatched bunch, and trying to explain what we were doing in the shipping lanes would not, I thought, be easy. But we were in the pirates' hands and didn't have much option other than to do what they suggested.

Not long after we set sail, it started to look as if our plan wasn't going to be successful. We were way out in the Malacca Straits – land had disappeared – when one of the many patrol boats turned towards us. It was painted in brown and blue camouflage, had a distinctly military look, and appeared to have clocked us.

I felt my heart sink. Associating with pirates was undoubtedly a serious offence, and a stint in an Indonesian jail wasn't very high up the list of things I wanted to do while I was here. Fortunately for us, at the last minute the patrol boat veered away. It seemed we were of no interest to it, and we were able to continue our voyage unobserved.

We steered into the path of what looked to me like a very large vessel. I asked Storm if he would consider pirating a ship that size. He nodded his head.

'Isn't it too high?' I asked him.

'No,' he replied emphatically. 'No, this is almost perfect.' He said he would take it from behind (no sniggering at the back), which surprised me because the freeboard was at its highest there. But what surprised me even more than that was the fact that as we were bobbing around in the ocean discussing the niceties of how to hijack a ship, the ship itself was heading straight for us. Because of our perspective, it was difficult to say just how fast the vessel was travelling, but it was certainly shifting – one moment it looked far away, and the next it was almost on top of us. Its bow wave and wake were massive – for a brief moment I got an insight into the nerves you'd need to get up close to one of these things when they're moving. What was clear, however, was that this big ship simply hadn't seen us. It was on a direct collision course and was making no attempt to steer away or to alert us to its presence. The implication wasn't lost on me: if this ship couldn't see us during the hours of daylight, what kind of chance would it have at night?

Storm reiterated that he had taken ships this size. 'For shopping,' he said.

Not for hijacking, though?

'Sometimes.'

Our little boat rolled and rattled in the wake. Wouldn't they wait until it was stationary, to make life a bit easier?

No way. 'Moving. While it's moving.'

We continued our tour of the shipping lanes and before long drew up alongside another vessel, the NYK *Antares*, 300 metres long and registered in Panama. It was piled high with countless enormous, colourful shipping containers – impossible to say what it was carrying, but it certainly had a lot of stuff on board. It was, Storm told me, an ideal target for shopping. This wasn't just because of its shape and size but because, as it came from Panama, its crew would most likely be carrying American dollars. As in so many other parts of the world, in Batam the greenback talks. Ships carrying dollars run a much higher risk of hit-and-run attacks than any others. Storm estimated that there would be a minimum of $3,000 on board. Three thousand bucks would go a long way in Batam, but our pirates told us that they wouldn't be satisfied with that as a payday. 'If they are only carrying the minimum then we have to find more boats,' Storm explained. 'In one night we aim to collect $15,000 before we go home.'

Fifteen thousand dollars. Hence the smart four-by-four parked outside his house. I wondered how often they would go out shopping to swipe sums like this. 'It's difficult to say. Sometimes we go out once a month, sometimes it's two or three times a month. We usually go shopping at the beginning of the month because that's when the crew get paid.' So, if nothing else, our boys knew how to get the maximum return on their investment. There was something extremely businesslike about the way they approached all this.

Unlike the previous vessel, the *Antares* spotted us. There was a man on the bridge wing with a pair of binoculars and a radio. He clearly didn't like what he saw. The air was suddenly filled with a huge sound. Many merchant vessels have the facility to operate directional horns, a piece of apparatus that they use in an attempt to prevent piracy. If I were a pirate, I could well imagine that having that number of decibels blasted in your direction could encourage you to try your luck elsewhere. Apparently, though, they're not all that effective.

On this occasion the noise was more than enough to warn us off. If we didn't move away they could easily have sent out a distress call, and in any case, if any of the patrol ships had heard the *Antares'* horn, they could well be in the vicinity soon.

'Turn away!' Storm shouted. '*Turn away!*' There was an edge to his voice, so we made ourselves scarce.

As the day progressed, Storm and Ghost continued to

point out vessels in the Malacca Straits. There barely seemed to be any that they wouldn't consider pirating. Many of the ships they showed us had high freeboards. I'd learned in Somalia that high-freeboard boats were generally less vulnerable because it was more difficult for the pirates to use their ladders and grappling hooks to get on deck. But these Indonesian pirates seemed confident – blasé, even – that they could board such vessels with ease. What was more amazing was that they didn't use ladders *or* grappling hooks. They had a different technique – one that had been used in this region for centuries.

But there wasn't time for them to tell me about it now. The sky was darkening. Clouds gathered. We had no lights on board, and because we were so small we were not identifiable on any ship's radar. This meant we were vulnerable to collisions, so with that thought in mind we decided to call it a day, and headed back to shore.

That night there was another torrential thunderstorm. The heavens opened. It had been a long old day, a day during which I'd had a small taste of what it was like to be a pirate on the Malacca Straits. Frankly, I was very glad to return to the relative comfort of a hotel room, rather than be stuck out at sea in a tiny rickety boat, buffeted by the billowing swell of the waves, the air almost as full of water as the wide, hazardous ocean.

14. Five Little Pirates Sitting in a Tree

There are certain things you never expect to hear yourself say. 'I'm glad I've bumped into pirates' is probably one of them. But after so much time searching, so many disappointments and shattered expectations, I was pretty pleased to have made contact with some genuine Indonesian pirates, to be shown the ropes by Storm and Ghost. And as they seemed to trust us, the next day they offered to take us out to an island where they would demonstrate to us the techniques they used to board ships. Just one problem: the island to which they were taking us was one of those that they used to maroon hijacked crews. I was glad that our investigation was bearing fruit, but I think it was at the back of everyone's mind that we needed to stay on the good side of these characters if we didn't want to be marooned ourselves . . .

The pirates had said that what they were about to show us required the use of parangs – a kind of machete that is very common in that part of the world. But for some bizarre legal or health and safety reason that I still don't understand, we were informed by London that I had to supply the weapons. Fortunately, getting your hands on a parang is rather easier on Batam island than it is back home – you just walk into a hardware store and pay your money. They even did me a deal – buy two, get a third off. In Indonesia parangs are everywhere – it's a bit like buying a screwdriver.

Except, of course, that a parang can do a lot more damage than a Phillips. In any case, when we finally hooked up with our pirates again, they already had their own machetes.

Hardware sorted, it was time to leave Batam. This time the pirates sent a boat for us. We loaded up and sped towards one of the many islands that are dotted around this stretch of water. As we travelled, the horizon was dominated by the skyline of Singapore and I was reminded once more what a temptation that must be for the poor people of Indonesia. With millions of dollars' worth of goods and cash sailing out of that port, right past their front door, it's hardly surprising that some of them grab the opportunity to fill their boots. And there were hundreds of islands too. If the pirates had a fast boat, they could squirrel themselves away on one of these islands and it would be virtually impossible to find them.

We had agreed with the pirates that we wouldn't reveal the name of the island they used for their activities. When we arrived there, the tide was out so our boat had to anchor several football pitches away from the shore. As a result we had to wade in with water up to our knees – a slightly nervy process because the region plays host to stone fish, highly poisonous ceatures which are able to camouflage themselves against the underwater stones. Stepping on one of those can be at best excruciating, at worst fatal. The locals were happy to take the risk; I wore my shoes. We must have been an odd sight, and the balaclava'd pirates waiting for us on the island – five or six of them on this occasion, members of Storm's crew – knew that. They stayed firmly out of sight, behind the treeline, in case we attracted any unwanted attention.

Bamboo grows high on this island, and it was among the bamboo that the pirates were waiting for us. This was the raw material of their trade, the thing they used to board ships in the absence of ladders and grappling hooks. Armed with super-sharp parangs – which they wielded with great skill – they cut down a 40- to 50-foot high bamboo stalk, before shaving off the sharp edges to leave a perfectly smooth pole. As they worked I noticed for the first time that almost to a man the skin on their legs was covered with indentations that looked as if they had been carved away with a teaspoon. This, I was told, was a result of scratching away at mosquito bites when they were children, and it was certainly true that the mosquito population was very high.

The pirates would use a bamboo pole such as they had just prepared to rest against the side of the ship, but in order for it to stay in place they needed some sort of hook at the top. I was expecting a dedicated metal hook; in fact they used a short, strong length of a particular root, which they tied to the end of the bamboo with twine (in a delightful shade of pink) and fixed in a V-shape so it could be used to hang the whole bamboo from the railing on the edge of a ship's deck.

The pirates made their bamboo poles from scratch in minutes. In order to scale a high-freeboard boat they would need to join a few such lengths of bamboo together, so it might take a little longer. But not much. I couldn't help wondering what would happen if they were caught travelling with a piece of equipment like this. Storm shrugged. 'Before the marine police catch us,' he said, 'we throw everything overboard. Into the sea.' Which made perfect sense, of course, because all they needed to do was come back here and make another one.

It was impressive stuff, but I still couldn't quite see how anyone could shimmy up it so they offered to show me. Obviously we couldn't do it out at sea because we'd be arrested; instead they hung the bamboo pole from the branch of a nearby tree. The base of the pole was a couple of metres from the ground; the top was several metres up. If I had tried to make like a pirate and climb the bamboo, everyone would have had a good laugh and I'd have landed in a heap. Not so these guys. With his parang slung across his back, the first one shimmied up the pole in moments. Then the next. Within seconds, there were five little pirates sitting in the tree. And if they could be up a tree in seconds, they could be on the deck of merchant vessel in seconds too.

The pirates slid back down as easily as they had shimmied up. Once they were on terra firma, Storm explained to me exactly what would happen once they had boarded the vessel. 'We take our parangs,' he said. 'We look for the crew on the ship and we apprehend them. We go directly to the bridge and turn off the communications system, then we look for the captain. I tell the captain I need money and it's better for him to surrender and not fight back. If you fight back, you're going to die.'

And if the captain says no?

'Then we have to hurt them.'

Generally speaking, Storm said, it was the Russian and Korean crews who tended to put up a struggle. If this should happen, they cut their victims' hands – he demonstrated with a mock slash across his palm. 'When their hand is wounded, they start bleeding, and when they see the blood, they usually give up.' And, of course, a man with sliced-up hands is severely disabled.

But what if their hostages still fight back?

'We kill him.'

Simple as that. Indeed, simplicity was the key to the pirates' endeavours – I doubted that the techniques they had shown me had changed for hundreds of years. If it ain't broke, don't fix it. The pink twine they used to attach the hook was a modern invention, but it would have been perfectly possible to use some sort of natural cordage in its place. It also struck me that their outlay was minimal. Storm said that they tended to hire boats from local smugglers, and the rest of the equipment they need is just there for the taking, with the exception of the parangs, which can be bought cheaply from a hardware store. It's not quite like having to get your hands on a sawn-off shotgun to commit an armed robbery. Expenditure tiny; potential rewards huge. No wonder Storm and his crew were eager practitioners of their art.

Before we left the island, the pirates used their parangs to hack up the bamboo stalks and hide their tracks. They were worried about the patrol boats in the area, so we decided to call it a day. As we headed back, we encountered yet another torrential Indonesian rainstorm, one of the worst I'd ever experienced. Forging across the water back towards Batam, I couldn't have been wetter if I'd jumped in the sea. In the distance, a huge, bright rainbow shone above one of the many islands, dipping over the horizon and back down into the sea. Was there a pot of gold at the end of it? I couldn't help thinking that if you were a pirate, armed only with a piece of bamboo and a razor-sharp parang, there probably was.

*

In our minds, pirates are mysterious, romantic figures. In reality, they're just ordinary people, criminals who ply their trade at sea. As such, they have ordinary concerns, and families too. I was given the opportunity to meet the wife of one of Storm's crew. Like her husband, the pirate's wife didn't want her face shown or her name revealed. Rather than don a makeshift balaclava, however, she hid her features more elegantly using a small umbrella as we sat by the waterfront and discussed what it was like to be married to the mob.

She was a lovely girl – softly spoken, heavily pregnant and with passable, if hesitant, English. She had met her husband nine years previously and for a while they were best friends. She came from a good background and explained that her family – many of whom had died in the Bali bombings – had no idea that she was married to a pirate. They all believed he earned his living from a small shop he owned, where he sold handmade chairs. I wondered what would happen if they found out the truth.

'They ask me to divorce, maybe.'

Even though the baby's on the way?

She nodded her head.

The pirate's wife explained to me that when Storm's crew went out on a job, the wives would all spend the night together in one house, trying to sleep but more often chatting and comforting each other as they waited for their husbands to come home safely. The worst times, she said, were when the men switched off their mobile phones. Out of sight. Out of contact. But not out of mind. I could only imagine the strain they must be under, knowing that their men were out doing something so potentially dangerous, knowing that they could disappear, or die. Who would look after her then, I asked.

She gave a little laugh. 'Nobody,' she replied.

Doesn't that worry her as well?

'Yeah, I worry. I say this one already to him, but he say, "This is my life. I had this one before I see you."'

It was in his blood, she told me, to be a pirate. 'Sometimes he say, "If I have a son, I want him same like me. Be the pirate."'

And would that make her happy too?

'No. I want he be the police. Maybe this is how to stop the father being a pirate.'

This young lady was under no illusions about the reality of her husband's activities. She surely knew that he could kill people – that maybe he had already. Did that not bother her? 'This is a problem for me,' she said, 'but I cannot say anything. This is his life.'

The pirate's wife clearly worried and disapproved of her husband's nocturnal activities. At the same time she accepted that this was how he brought home the bacon. 'We eat from this job,' she said quietly. 'If he not go for working, we no have anything.'

She was very frank with me, and the more we spoke the more I realized that her life was very far from being a bed of roses. Her husband clearly liked life in the fast lane, and that wasn't limited to piracy. 'Girls, money, drugs – all the pirates same like that.' Even her husband? 'Now after married, no – but before he always drunk. If he drink, he always slap me, fight with me, hit me. After he know I'm pregnant, he change everything. But I know him. He's not a good man. He's a naughty boy.'

There was something slightly tragic about her. Without wanting to over-romanticize it, I was reminded of Carmela Soprano. She wasn't a bad person; she was just resigned to the reality of her life. She didn't want her husband to be a pirate, but she knew she couldn't change him. Maybe she didn't *want* to change him. There was a curious mixture of disapproval and acceptance, and it all came down to the age-old story. Before they got married, her husband's family gave her the third degree.

'They say, "Do you know he no go to school?"'

'I say, "Yeah, I know."'

'"Do you know he the pirate? Do you know he stay in jail before?"'

'And I say, "Yeah, I know."'

'"And you accept him?"'

'"If he accept me, I can accept everything, bad and good, from him. Because I love him."'

It was abundantly clear that this young woman was not with her husband for any reason other than love. 'For me, money not mean anything. If you have love, maybe you can have anything you want.'

And maybe you can. But as the sun went down over the seas where her husband plied his dangerous trade, I couldn't help wondering what the future held for this quietly spoken woman, pregnant by a pirate she loved and unable – perhaps unwilling – to get him to change his ways.

My time on the island of Batam was drawing to a close. But before I left I took the opportunity to meet Storm and his crew one last time. They had shown me *where* they performed their acts of piracy; they had shown me *how* they performed their acts of piracy. But so far they hadn't been too forthcoming on the whys and wherefores. We met on yet another island – the lads had even put on fresh balaclavas for the occasion – and as we sat under a tree, shading ourselves from the blistering heat of the Indonesian sun, I tried to get to the bottom of why these pirates did what they did.

'Poverty is everywhere,' Storm told me. 'We steal to eat, not to get rich.'

Really? I put it to them that when they go shopping, they can make a lot of money in one night. Storm disagreed. 'When we go shopping we find that not every ship has a lot of cash. So if we don't get much we have to do it again until we get at least $10,000 each and then we go home.'

I wasn't quite buying it. They said they only committed acts of piracy to eat, not to get rich. But that kind of money buys a lot of food. I suggested to them that it also buys cars and houses.

A beat.

An unpleasant silence.

Up until now the atmosphere between me and Storm's crew had been good. Relaxed even. This was the only time it turned. They obviously didn't like the way the conversation had gone, and suddenly the mood changed, like a cloud slipping over the sun. I knew that I couldn't afford to upset them too much – if things became nasty between us, they could just mug us, steal our camera equipment and leave us on the island.

Storm shook his head. 'No,' he said. And that was that. He didn't want to elaborate, and I certainly wasn't going to push the issue.

We'd heard rumours that there was a mythology among Indonesian pirates that they could make themselves invisible. Not normally the sort of thing you'd give credence to, but after my experiences in Nigeria I was interested to know what Storm and the crew had to say. One of the younger members, whose ears made his balaclava stick out comically, put his oar in. 'That's right,' he announced. 'We have supernatural powers. You can call it magic. We make people see other things instead of us. For example, for two months I went shopping every day and I was never caught. So I believe it.'

He spoke passionately. His mates, though, were on the verge of laughter. I asked Storm what he thought. 'I used to believe it,' he admitted. 'But then I was caught and put in jail!'

Ah.

'So I don't believe in magic any more. I use common sense now.'

Common sense sounded to me like a better strategy than mysticism. The guys told me that the brother of one of them was a member of the maritime police, and he knew full well how his sibling made his living. The two brothers had an agreement: if the copper had to nick the pirate, he would go to jail; but in the meantime he agreed not to shop him. Like I say: common sense, not magic.

Given that most of the crew didn't consider themselves to be invulnerable, however, didn't they worry that one day they'd be caught or would come to harm? 'That's always a risk in this kind of job,' one of the crew admitted. 'We don't think about life and death. We die when the time comes for us to die. That's the risk we choose to take.'

The vibe between us all had settled down now. I felt a bit more comfortable asking my last question of this gang of pirates. 'What would happen if someone tried to give away your identity? If a pirate went to the police, what would happen to him?'

A pregnant pause.

'Our law is Mafia law,' answered Ghost. 'We would kill that person.'

And as if to back him up, another repeated the words.

'Kill him,' he said.

We took our leave of the pirates. They didn't, in the end, maroon us, or rob us. They just disappeared, unrepentant and proud, ready to steal another day. I prepared to leave Batam – and south-east Asia – with the strange feeling that always accompanies meeting people like that. I knew they were criminals. I knew that what they did was wrong. I didn't condone it in any way. But when you get to know people on a personal level, you can't help but start to understand things from their point of view. Storm and his crew claimed to be driven by poverty. How true that was, I can't say. He certainly seemed to live in a nicer house than most, and he drove a decent car. The sort of sums they claimed to secure when they went shopping were substantial – enough to keep more people than just them well clear of the breadline. And though Batam was a notorious pirate hot spot, there were plenty of poor people there who *didn't* resort to illegality.

That said, Storm and his boys were hardly living a life of unparalleled luxury. If they weren't able to earn their living from piracy, what sort of life *would* they have? Indonesia is a poor country. Nearly 18 per cent of its people live below the poverty line, and nearly 50 per cent live on less than two dollars a day. It's not difficult to see why crime might thrive; and in a country that is made up of thousands of tiny islands, it's not difficult to see why a substantial proportion of that crime might take place on the water – especially in an area where they have the imposing skyline of rich Singapore to tempt them. I didn't admire the pirates for their violence, but I did have a sneaking admiration for their focus and professionalism, for making their difficult way in a difficult world.

Moreover, by their own admission, the people I had met were very much on the bottom rung of piracy. They weren't commanding multi-million-dollar ransoms like the Somali pirates, and they were being manipulated by shadowy Mr Big figures who were pocketing the real money while Storm's crew risked their lives and their liberty. It was the Mr Bigs that I really despised, not their foot soldiers.

I didn't leave Batam feeling sympathy for the pirates I had met, but I did feel I understood them. And I also understood this. Piracy at sea is not so different from criminality on land. It will exist as long as the gulf between the haves and the have-nots remains wide.

PART 4
Djibouti

15. The Pirate of Puntland

While I had been in south-east Asia, piracy off the coast of Somalia had gone off the scale. During my time on HMS *Northumberland* a delicate kind of ceasefire had existed. The warships of Operation Atalanta had refrained from storming hijacked ships; in return, the pirates had held back from killing their hostages. But since then things had changed, and they'd changed for the worse.

The *Maersk Alabama* was a 17,000-tonne American cargo ship. It was attacked by four pirates in the April of 2009, but things did not go quite according to their plan. When the pirates boarded, the captain, Richard Phillips, instructed all his crew to lock themselves in their cabins. He then offered himself to the pirates as a hostage, with the proviso that the *Alabama* was set free. The pirates put Phillips on one of the merchant vessel's bright-orange lifeboats, then sailed it to within 30 miles of the Somali coast under the constant surveillance of US warships and helicopters.

FBI hostage negotiators flew to the scene and opened up lines of communication. The pirates demanded a ransom of $2 million in return for the captain's life. The captain tried to escape by jumping into the sea. The pirates easily recaptured him – though one of them sustained an injury to his hand – and started making threats against his life. They were surrounded by the might of the American navy, including the missile cruiser USS *Bainbridge*, but that didn't seem to dampen their enthusiasm.

Days passed. The pirates ran out of food and water. They accepted supplies from the Americans, and as a result a small boat made several trips between the pirates and the *Bainbridge*. On one of these trips the pirate with the wounded hand asked for medical assistance. He was, in effect, surrendering, and he was taken back to the American warship.

That left three of them, and Captain Phillips.

Unbeknown to the pirates, a team of US Navy Seals had parachuted into the sea with inflatable boats before being picked up by the *Bainbridge*. Their orders, direct from President Obama, were to use force only if Captain Phillips' life appeared to be in imminent danger. Four days after their original attack the pirates, having run out of fuel, accepted a towline from the *Bainbridge*. That evening, however, the Seals observed a tracer bullet coming from the pirates' boat. Tracers are generally only fired in order to give the user an idea of the trajectory on which they should fire live rounds. It didn't exactly ease the tension, and the Seals used night-vision devices to see what was happening. One of the pirates, they observed, had his assault rifle pointed at the back of Captain Phillips; what was more, the Seals had a clear line of fire at all three targets.

The Seals received the order to fire. Three pirates. Three shots. That was all they needed, even though the lifeboat was being trailed at the end of a 100-foot line and presented a moving target for the sharpshooters. The pirates died instantly and the Seals rescued Captain Phillips.

The *Maersk Alabama* was the first American ship to be pirated since the Second Barbary War nearly 200 years previously, and the reaction to the death of the pirates on the Somali mainland showed the problems involved with using military force to combat piracy. A pirate holding a Greek ship went on the record as saying, 'Every country will be treated the way it treats us. In the future, America will be the one crying . . .'

Intervention by special forces led to the pirates being killed and Captain Phillips being rescued. But the good guys don't always win, no matter how highly trained they are; violence doesn't always go according to plan. This was well illustrated by an incident that occurred at practically the same time as the hijacking of the *Maersk Alabama*. This was the pirating of the French yacht *Tanit*. The *Tanit*'s skipper was a 28-year-old man by the name of Florent Lemacon, and on board were four other passengers, including his wife and three-year-old son.

Lemacon was making his way down the Gulf of Aden to the island of Zanzibar, off the coast of Tanzania. He'd been warned about the dangers, but had made the decision not to heed the advice – by all accounts he was a free spirit, determined not to allow criminal elements to stop him from going where and doing what he wanted. Good on him, I guess. They took certain precautions, such as sailing with their lights dimmed to avoid detection by pirates. They even sent a message from the middle of the ocean which read, 'We are in the middle of the piracy zone . . . the danger is there, and has indeed become greater over the past months, but the ocean is vast. The pirates must not be allowed to destroy our dream.'

Unfortunately, the pirates didn't see it quite the same way. *Tanit* was 400 miles off the coast of Somalia when it was boarded by pirates with AK-47s and held to ransom. Unfortunately for the Lemacons, they didn't have the might of an international shipping organization behind them, nor a precious cargo – at least not in monetary terms. Negotiations with the pirates broke down. On this occasion there was no suitcase full of used notes parachuted onto the deck. Instead, there was a troop of French special forces, dispatched to do what special forces do.

The commandos stormed the yacht and were engaged by the gun-toting pirates. A firefight took place, and two of the pirates were killed. But the yacht's skipper was caught in the crossfire and took a bullet in the head. Whether it came from a pirate's gun or from one of the French SF weapons isn't public knowledge. The net result was the same, though: Florent Lemacon died instantly, widowing a wife and orphaning a child.

The significance of these two events wasn't lost on me. During my stay on HMS *Northumberland* the Royal Marines had been unable to board the pirated *Saldanha* for fear that the pirates, who so far had avoided killing their hostages, would change tack. The Somali pirates certainly had the weaponry to cause a great deal of death and destruction, and if the situation on the mainland was anything to go by, they were ruthless enough to do so should they decide to. The question was this: now that foreign governments had started to retaliate, would the pirates escalate the situation? Was the body count about to start rising?

My time on *Northumberland* had been interesting but ultimately frustrating. I still felt there was more to learn about the situation in Somalia, that there was more of a story to tell. Of course, nothing had changed on the mainland – setting foot on Somali soil was still so hazardous as to make it a no-go area for Western film crews. We could, however, go back to Djibouti, the neighbouring country where we had disembarked from *Northumberland*. Which was handy, because we had an in with a fixer who was about to put a cherry on the top of the cake of our investigation.

His name wasn't Jacques, but that's what I'll call him. He was a good-looking Frenchman who ran a diving school in that tiny country. My impression was that he was a man with connections – a good pair of eyes and a brain full of local knowledge that he would share with anyone for a fee. He knew everyone, and everyone knew Jacques. Djibouti is now a military port, and while we were there a Japanese warship arrived. The commander sought Jacques out and asked if he could help him go hunting for big game. Perhaps he had mistaken Djibouti for the Serengeti.

Jacques' face was a picture. 'You are mad!' he said. 'You want to kill things? There's nothing to kill here. I can take you diving, but you cannot kill anything.' The commander was sent packing, disappointed that he wasn't able to decorate the bridge of his ship with a rhino's head; but happily Jacques was of more use to us in the hunt for our quarry. He knew people who knew people, and thought he could fix us up with a genuine Somali pirate. It was too good an opportunity to pass up.

Jacques specialized in getting people in and out of Somalia, and said that he could, in principle, get us into the piratical region of Puntland. Like everyone else we talked to, though, he qualified his statement by saying we only had a 50-50 chance of getting out alive. Camera teams, he told us, were especially at risk. If you went into Somalia as a fixer or a problem solver and got killed, chances were there would be repercussions from your murder from whoever was hiring you. But camera teams don't go into that country at anyone's behest. Nobody in Somalia is going to protect them. If we wanted to meet Jacques' pirate *in* Somalia, the only way of doing it would be to fly into a provincial Puntland airport and conduct the interview on the tarmac. That might be all right, but Jacques also told us that if we chose that option, we'd have to make sure our plane's engines were constantly turning over. Great for a quick getaway if everything went pear-shaped; impossible for our camera crew to record anything satisfactory above the sound of the engines.

We couldn't travel to meet Jacques' pirate for all these reasons. But maybe he could fix it so that the pirate could come to us. Only time would tell. Meanwhile we had another stroke of good luck.

Colonel Abshir was born in the Bari region of northern Somalia. Having passed through the Somali Military Academy, where he studied tanks, army fighting and military leadership, he became a lieutenant colonel and a high-ranking intelligence officer in the government of Siad Barré – the last Somali administration to be officially recognized by the international community. Some people branded Barré's regime a dictatorship; I could only imagine what an intelligence officer in such a regime had got up to. Barré was removed from power in a coup and died in Kenya in 1995, but former members of his government remained influential in Somali society, and Colonel Abshir was one of them. He was now part of the Puntland Private Security Consultation Organization. As such, he knew a thing or two about the pirates of Puntland. We had arranged to meet him in Djibouti, to get an insight into Somali piracy from someone on the inside.

It was a hot, dusty afternoon. Impossibly hot – the kind of heat that you know will do you damage if you stay out in it too long. We met in a room at Jacques' diving school.

As we sat down together in the blistering heat, Colonel Abshir told me of his hopes for his country. 'I was born in an independent Somalia,' he said. 'There was a central government that was governing the whole country. My only wish is to see a proper Somali central government, a government with proper institutions that safeguards law and order and wipes out the current situations of sea piracy, terrorism and other problems, and provides a proper, lasting solution for Somalia. My ambition is to have a peaceful life. For the remaining days of my life, I would like to live in Somalia with a government that offers me and my family the opportunity to get education, employment and guaranteed security for the future. I wish to have a government that is good to its neighbouring countries and the entire world. God willing, that will happen one day.'

God willing indeed. But the gulf between the Somalia of Colonel Abshir's ambitions and the one that currently existed seemed to me to be almost insurmountably wide.

I wanted to talk to the colonel about what I'd heard regarding the reasons for piracy in Somalia – the toxic waste, the illegal fishing. His answer was not quite what I expected. 'Yes,' he said, 'there is dumping of material such as nuclear waste, industrial waste, illegal fishing in our waters and other problems. However, the simple, ordinary pirate boy has no knowledge of these. It is not, as they claim, that they are patriotic and defending the fishes in our sea or against waste and other illegal activities. These illiterate pirates have no knowledge of what nuclear or industrial waste *is*. These pirates are employees, and are put to work by some individuals.'

The colonel's point was enlightening. I didn't have much doubt that the dumping of toxic waste and the illegal fishing of Somali waters had been at least a catalyst for the piracy that currently existed, but what he seemed to be saying was that it had now evolved into something more businesslike.

What of Eyl, that lawless pirate town to which the MV *Saldanha* had been taken. 'Eyl is the garage of hijacked ships,' he agreed. 'The pirate will take the kidnapped ship to Eyl because in there he will find his friends, plenty of other sea pirates who are also armed and live in Eyl.'

I asked him how he expected the use of force in the cases of the *Maersk Alabama* and the *Tanit* to affect piracy in the region. 'From now on,' he told me, 'I think that if a French or American national is taken hostage, they won't ask for a ransom. They will either give them back or treat them in the same way that their friends were treated.'

Treating them in the same way, of course, meant shooting them. I couldn't help but think that this was a more likely outcome than simply letting them go.

Abshir smiled as he spoke. It was difficult to judge quite what he thought about all this. 'The pirates,' he told me, 'are like a family, regardless of where they come from. They share a common interest.'

And family, as we know, look after their own.

Colonel Abshir revealed to me the Somali pirates were not working entirely on their own – some of them were getting outside help. 'We know that there are some nationals from Sudan, Asmara, Mombasa that are helping pirates, teaching them techniques.' (Sudan! Perhaps my slip of the tongue when I was pontificating for the chiefs of Ajegunle hadn't been so wide of the mark . . .) In fact, the problem went deeper than that. 'During the war between the two Yemens, which North Yemen won, there were many military officers from the south who were sacked from their jobs. These officers were disarmed and suffered demoralization. They were later given some small fishing boats. They used to fish in the Somali water and had a good working relationship with other Somali fishermen. We know that they are now involved in the piracy in Somalia. I have concrete evidence of a case in which some Yemeni fishermen from the former marine force of Yemen actually hijacked a ship and sold it to the Somali pirates.'

From what the colonel was saying, the problem of piracy off the coast of Somalia was more multi-layered than I had previously thought. There were the fishermen; there were the people who controlled the fishermen; there were foreigners who had been attracted to the region because of unrest in their own countries. I wondered if Abshir had any idea of the number of pirates currently operating in his country. 'Our organization,' he told me, 'has registered the number of pirates to be nearly 3,000.' This figure included both those who had actually taken part in acts of piracy as well as those who were dealers and investors. Amazingly, Colonel Abshir claimed to know exactly who they all were. 'We have registered all of them and have photographs of most of them. We also have details of their names, ethnic origins, names of their mothers and their places of birth and nationality. We monitor their activities and know their current situations – where they are and if they have left the country.'

If this was true, it was astonishing. In Nigeria and Batam the pirates were shadowy and secretive. In Somalia, apparently, the authorities had their numbers, but because of the disastrous situation in that country, they were powerless to act. 'I can't give their names at the moment,' Abshir said, 'because they are too powerful.'

I could understand that the colonel might not want to give us the names of those people he knew to be involved in piracy. That could be dangerous for his health. But I did want to know what was happening to the massive quantities of money that were being earned as ransoms for the merchant vessels taken to Eyl. 'The team on the ship share the money,' he told me, 'and the biggest share goes to the boss.' And these bosses, he said, were very, very wealthy men. 'Millionaires. *Millionaires!*'

The big question was this: how do you stop someone from becoming a pirate? 'If all the warships in the world were gathered together in the Somali sea,' he suggested, 'it's still not a solution.' My time on *Northumberland* suggested he was right. And he predicted that if things continued on their current trajectory, the situation could only get worse. 'If the international community chooses not to do anything, it is possible that these movements of piracy, terrorism, smugglers, illegal armies, drug traffickers and human rights abuses could lead to worse international security situations. Everything that is possible will happen. There could be explosions. They could explode oil tankers. They could even kill people on captured ships because the pirates now have enough money and are very rich. They might not need any more money. That is possible.'

And did the colonel have any suggestions as to how the international community could help?

'Only if they could approach the small regional administration of Puntland, offer to recruit and train one to two thousand soldiers from the Somalis in Puntland, offer proper equipment, install intelligence systems and also offer financial assistance to Puntland. I strongly believe that the budget of all that will be less than what they are now spending on a half-day. If they could make a network and launch one very successful operation against these pirates, I am sure they would be wiped out.'

Not the worst idea I'd ever heard. But as the colonel spoke I couldn't help remembering that the international community had tried to intervene in Somalia before. The result of that intervention had been the disastrous Battle of Mogadishu. I didn't doubt that Abshir's belief that piracy needed to be tackled on land, not at sea, was on the money. But having been bitten once, I can't help thinking that the international community is likely to be twice shy . . .

Colonel Abshir's take on Somalian piracy had been bleak but honest. However, I was about to get a much more personal view of the situation. Because finally, after months of searching, the call finally came in. By ways and means that I can't fully reveal, our contacts had come good. A meet had been arranged and we were about to come face to face with a genuine Somali pirate, one of the reckless individuals who wreak such havoc in the Gulf of Aden, commanding ransoms of millions of pounds, and striking genuine fear into the hearts of any ships' crews passing through that busy and important waterway.

We were told to leave the city of Djibouti and travel by boat to a secret location – a small island just off the coast and not far from Somali waters. It was early in the morning, but already the heat was intense. The waters round the island were crystalline and blue – like something out of a holiday brochure. I wouldn't recommend taking your holidays round here, though, for fear of encountering someone like the man I was here to meet. We stood on the sandy shore of that island, not knowing what to expect or even if our man was actually going to turn up for sure. After my experiences in Nigeria I was more than prepared to be disappointed yet again. Pirates, I had learned, had a way of promising one thing and doing another. Reliability was not their strong point.

But then, as I stood on the beach, a boat slid slowly into view.

It was a small boat. Old. Painted white, with an outboard motor. There were two men in it, dark-skinned and with black and white keffiyehs wrapped around their heads to obscure their faces. One of these men was our pirate. He wore a white short-sleeved shirt and dark trousers. His body was thin – slight almost. In many ways he was unremarkable to look at. Unprepossessing. As we settled down to talk on the beach, I had the impression that he was rather bemused by my interest in him and the way he made his living, as though sea piracy was rather run-of-the-mill. The norm. At the same time he seemed aware of the image that Somali pirates had around the world – especially since the hijacking of the *Tanit* and the *Alabama* – and he wanted to put his side of the story.

I asked him how he became a pirate and he explained that he used to be a fisherman. 'The community faced difficulties,' he told me, 'because the fishermen were chased away from the sea by the invasion of illegal fishing. The problem started because of the invasion and the fighting began. When they destroyed our fishing nets with fishes inside, then we started fighting them.'

Colonel Abshir had told me that the pirates of Somalia were illiterates who had no idea of illegal fishing and toxic waste. This man admitted to me that he was indeed illiterate, but he certainly knew something of the origins of piracy in the area. As he spoke, though, it became clear that it had definitely evolved into something bigger. Our pirate did not work for himself. He was bankrolled by someone further up the line. An investor. A Mr Big. When a ransom was collected successfully, he told me, the pirates would get 30 per cent, Mr Big would get 70 per cent. A disproportionate cut but still – 30 per cent of a few million goes a long way in Somalia. 'It's true,' he said. 'There are some who are very rich. Everywhere you go, people welcome you because they say you have a lot of money, and they receive you warmly.'

What did the pirates do with that sort of money?

'We use it to build houses,' he told me. 'We give half to our families and the other half we spend on our relatives, who could be in the town or the countryside.' Some of the money, he told me, he used to buy herds of camels – camel meat being much prized as a food in Somalia.

I asked our pirate to talk me through the process of capturing a ship. How did they go about it? What techniques did they use?

'We have some satellite radios that we use for communication,' he explained. 'We speak to the ship and order it to stop. If it does not stop, we open fire and eventually stop it by force. A ship carrying heavy cargo can be captured in less than five minutes. First we enter the ship and order all the persons on board to stand still. Then we anchor it. We install communication systems and communicate with the owner of the ship. We ask for the ransom money and tell them that we will hold the ship until the demand is met.'

He made it sound simple, and in a way, I suppose, it was. 'A ship has nothing to defend itself with,' he explained. 'Nothing!' I asked him what sort of weapons they used. He favoured an AK-47; others, he told me, were partial to the PKM – a Russian general purpose machine gun. Professional equipment for a professional job, most of which, he told me, came into the country from Ethiopia. But he qualified this. 'You can only use your weapon to defend against someone who attacks you. You do not need to use it for other purposes. Nobody just opens fire and wants to waste bullets.'

I thought of Storm and of his assertion that the Somali pirate is a stupid pirate. I wasn't sure I agreed. This guy sounded like he knew what he was talking about. Like he had it all worked out.

Abshir had predicted an escalation of violence, and I wondered what our pirate's take on the recent shootings aboard the *Maersk Alabama* and the *Tanit* heralded. Had the situation changed now that the Americans and French had killed Somali pirates? 'If a person enters our territory,' he said calmly, 'he won't be killed. But the French and Americans have caused problems by killing our people. Others will not be killed. We will contact their government to tell them that we have taken some of their nationals as hostages and tell them to come to Puntland to sort the matter out.' He clapped his hands together, almost as if he was relishing the prospect. It would be a brave foreign official, I thought, that would take him up on his offer . . .

I wanted to know how our man had become a pirate, how he had learned the techniques necessary to perform such audacious acts. The answer truly surprised me. 'If a person lives by the sea,' he said, 'and has sailed many times, then he can learn to be a pirate. You can learn piracy if you have your own gun and know how to defend yourself. There's nothing difficult about being at sea. If you're well trained you can do anything you want.'

But if you're well trained, that means somebody has trained you.

He nodded his head. 'Yes. I received a little training. There are about 30 schools for sea piracy in Somalia.'

Thirty schools. I had no idea if he was telling the truth, but if our pirate was alleging thirty, there's definitely more than one.

'The training takes about a year. They teach how to capture the ship, resolve the problems and how to keep the ship. They teach us about every sort of weapon – rocket-propelled grenades, anti-aircraft missiles and many other types.'

And who was it that was giving them this training?

'Our trainers are ex-marines, people who used to be in the Somali military.'

Someone, though, must be paying for all this. Our pirate nodded, before explaining that what often happens is this:

the big bosses pay for the pirates to undergo their year's training. Then, when the pirates start making money, they pay their bankrollers back. Student loans, Somalia style.

I asked him if he thought piracy would ever stop in Somalia. Again he nodded. 'If we get a proper government, then sea piracy will stop.' That, at least, seemed to be something everybody could agree on.

Our interview was drawing to a close. There was one more question I wanted to ask him. 'In other countries,' I suggested, 'you might be perceived to be criminals. How do you answer that?'

He looked genuinely astonished by the suggestion. 'Who?' he asked. 'Me? I am not a criminal and I have not committed any crime. And I've never hurt a white man.' He slapped his hands together again, as if to say that's that. But that final assertion begged the question: how many men had he hurt that didn't happen to be white?

And so our conversation came to an end. I thanked the pirate for agreeing to talk to me, and he told me that I would always be welcome in Somalia.

I appreciated the thought, and I'd never say never. But as the pirate from Puntland disappeared from view, his old white boat slipping over the horizon of that clear blue sea, I reflected on this: from what I knew about his ravaged, dangerous, violent country, I couldn't see that happening for a very long time to come.

Afterword

When I set out to investigate modern-day piracy, I didn't really know what I'd find. The things I discovered truly opened my eyes.

Piracy, it seems to me, exists for three reasons: criminal, economic and political. Sometimes the boundaries between these three reasons become blurred. Many criminals commit acts of villainy because they have an economic imperative, because they are poor. And many people are poor because of the terrible political situations in their country. What is undoubtedly the case is that it's not easy to make absolute judgements about the causes of piracy. And there are no easy solutions.

In Somalia I heard it said that piracy was the direct result of illegal fishing and the dumping of toxic waste, but it was also clear that there was a booming piratical business from which a lot of people were making a lot of money. In Nigeria there was some piracy that was clearly a direct result of economic hardship and some that was politically motivated, but on the other side of the fence there were plenty of people who saw MEND as out-and-out criminals. No doubt some of them were. The pirates of Batam claimed to go shopping simply to put food on the table for themselves and their families; while it was true that some of them drove big cars and had decent houses, you had to wonder whether they would have been forced into criminality had it not been for Indonesia's economic shape.

It was always touch and go that I would ever meet any actual pirates. I was glad I did, but in the end I was aware that the people I spoke to were little more than foot soldiers. The pirates themselves – the ones who take the risks and face the dangers – are just the tip of the iceberg. They are backed up by greater forces. The pirate from Puntland told us that 70 per cent of the takings from a ransomed ship went to these Mr Big figures, sponsors who paid for their training, expected their cut in return and had now grown filthy rich. In Nigeria small-time pirates were bunkering oil, but it was the people in authority – government ministers and wealthy businessmen – who were putting the oil onto the open market and reaping the substantial rewards. And in south-east Asia shipowners were hiring pirates to hijack their own vessels, often with the complicity of some of the crew, as part of elaborate and massive insurance scams.

Many merchant vessels around the world fly flags of convenience. This means that they originate from one country but are registered in another in order to attract a lower tax liability. When these ships get into trouble, however, they expect the maritime forces of the international community to come to their rescue. Whether you think that's acceptable or not, one thing is clear: piracy itself cannot be effectively policed. In Somalia a merchant vessel was taken from under our noses despite the impressive military presence of Operation Atalanta. If pirates don't fear a Type 23 frigate, they don't fear anything. In the Malacca Straits the efforts of the MMEA were having some effect, but the truth is that if you eliminate pirates from one stretch of water, all that happens is that they reappear somewhere else. If you look at maps indicating global piracy hot spots from year to year, you'll see that they change position, but they don't become noticeably less numerous.

Piracy, it seems to me, can't be stopped on the water. The sea is too big; the pirates' ships are too small; they can hide too easily; and once they've jettisoned the tools of their trade it's too difficult to distinguish them from fishermen. But 90 per cent of world trade travels by sea, and the problem has to be addressed. Piracy has existed ever since man first took to the water, and it would be naive to imagine we can eradicate it completely, but it's on the increase, and that worrying trajectory has to be reversed.

Maybe if we turned our eyes towards what is happening on the land, and focus on the *causes* of piracy, we might have a better chance of stopping it. Pirates aren't born at sea. They come from the land, they return to the land, and the money they spend, they spend on the land. Piracy is a seaborne menace that has its roots in poverty and political unrest on land. And as long as these continue, pirates will always take to the sea.

While people starve and governments fail their citizens, the waters of the world can never be safe.